Contents

Introduction

The main purpose of dress is to reveal.—The Connoisseur, 1755.

2. Adam and Eve. From the design on a "blue dash" charger of Bristol Delft ware. *A. F. Allbrook.*

Art is the use of material things to express ideas. In the art of costume the nature of the materials, their form and colour, combine to indicate, mostly by symbols, the ideas principally of social rank, occupation, and sex appeal.

For centuries this art has flourished without the guidance of Old Masters, quietly developing in the hands of all who chose their clothes for other reasons than just utility, unaware that in dressing themselves they were composing a work of art. Although each person seeks to impress something of his own personality on the costume he wears, posterity will find it less expressive of himself than of his group; it tells of a fashion rather than of a person.

A series of costumes illustrating the modes of past centuries reveals that rank has always been expressed by garments entailing varying degrees of physical discomfort —the higher the rank the greater the discomfort—combined with devices for limiting the movements of various joints, with men especially the neck, with women the trunk. These features are still preserved in ceremonial costume.

Sex appeal has been fortified by maintaining a marked difference between the costumes of the sexes. In women's there has been for the last six centuries a perpetual oscillation between concealment and exposure of regions having secondary sexual characteristics. Devices, no matter how uncomfortable or inconvenient, have been welcomed if it was thought that they might add an iota of sex appeal.

Although male fashions have been more concerned to express social class and female fashions to express sex appeal, it is common to find in the one a reflection of the other. Any fundamental change of design has usually appeared first in the male costume, followed after an interval in the female, and there carried to an extreme. Men's fashions have been the more original, women's the more imitative. In the last two centuries women had perpetually revived fashions of the past, men never.

A series of illustrations going back a thousand years or so reveals the development of the art. What had been the wrappings became, as it were, the very canvas of the picture, a medium for expressing the refinements of civilization as well as its cruder passions; an art so fascinating that men and women will make immense sacrifices in order to become its slaves.

The range of the art has expanded especially in the last hundred years by the introduction of the idea of aptness— that a costume shall suit the particular function in view— a notion accepted by civilized communities only with the greatest reluctance. Until quite recently soldiers were sent to fight in costumes ludicrously inappropriate to the battlefield, while the ban of public morality barred attempts to rationalize civilian dress, especially of the Upper Classes.

The first stage in the "functional" process was in the use of materials. For centuries wool had been shunned by the fashionable world as too "common", but early in the seventeenth century it was accepted as a material fit for gentlemen's suits, though not for ladies' dresses until the nineteenth century. Late in the eighteenth century male costume began to change from a pictorial design to one essentially architectural, a radical idea copied by women a century later in their "tailor-made" costume. This new conception of costume, with its variations of design to suit different functions, tended to obliterate the old distinctions of class, a process of rationalization as yet incomplete.

Viewing the costumes favoured by our ancestors we cannot but notice their apparent indifference to aesthetics. Harmony and discord, symmetry and distortion, tumbled over each other in successive fashions, all of which were thought beautiful by one generation and scorned by the next. Evidently in the art of costume beauty is irrelevant; significance is what counts. Those strange garments were thought by the wearers to be the very perfection of suitability and good taste. They seem strange to us only because the ideas they expressed seem strange.

PART ONE

The Middle Ages

The late Saxon costume still bore traces of the Classical style of dress, being, for both sexes, a loose covering concealing the shape of the body. It comprised, for men, a loose-sleeved Tunic, knee-length or ankle-length, under

c. 1370. A carved wooden figure said to be the angel Gabriel in a fitting kirtle with belt worn round the hips; long tight sleeves with buttons from the elbows to wrists. Mantle fastened across the chest. Chaplet on the head and hair flowing loose. This long kirtle style was usually a woman's dress. *Vicar's Choral, Wells.*

a sleeved Super-tunic or "Roc" (Saxon: hence "frock"), which was slightly shorter. A square Mantle or Cloak was an additional garment. A shirt was the only undergarment. The legs were clothed in Braies or loose-fitting drawers, ending above or below the knees, with long or short stockings. Alternatively, long drawers ("trousers"), ankle-length, might be worn with socks. Leg bandages like puttees were worn from knee to ankle either over the stockings or replacing them. Heel-less ankle boots or boots up to the mid-calf were worn out of doors.

Women's costume was basically very similar: a sleeved Tunic and Super-tunic (to the ground) commonly embroidered. A large square mantle and a head-rail (veil), the latter in the shape of a long broad scarf, the ends reaching the knees, draped the head and shoulders and concealed the hair.

The Norman tunic for men fitted the body slightly closer, while the female tunic, known as a Kirtle or Gown, was always worn with a girdle and under a Super-tunic. The head-rail became known as a Coverchief or Kerchief. The male costume, however dignified in repose, seems singularly unsuited for physical activities (a feature noticeable throughout the Middle Ages). The twelfth century introduced variations in the Tunic, the body sometimes close-fitting, the front of the skirt slit up, and the sleeves often short; at the same time the Braies shortened, becoming an undergarment.

A significant feature in women's dress began to appear after *c.* 1130, when ladies of rank assumed a gown moulded to the figure with tight sleeves adorned with pendulous cuffs; with it a long decorative girdle and embroidered shoes. More attention also was being paid to the head, with a wimple draped over the neck and bosom, while ladies of high rank allowed plaits of hair to descend in front.

The thirteenth century introduced sleeves of the male tunic ("Cote") made in one with the body with a wide armhole, while the Super-tunic or Surcote might be sleeveless (the "Tabard") or have wide tubular sleeves in a voluminous garment known as the Garde-corps, or Herigaut. Gloves were beginning to be fashionable.

The female Gown, known as a Kirtle, was long and trained, its neckline either cut lower or with a short V-opening closed by a brooch; the sleeves fitting or loose; a girdle round the waist. Both sexes had Fichets (vertical slits in the front of the Super-tunic or Kirtle) through which the purse, slung round the waist, could be reached.

About 1330 a radical change of idea began to assert itself in the costumes of both sexes. We might almost call it the dawn of modern costume, appearing all over Christendom but not elsewhere; the idea that the sexual features of the body, hitherto veiled in loose flowing garments, might be indicated by a closer fit. Henceforth, the dress of each sex became distinctive except in certain ceremonial forms when men as well as women wore long flowing "gowns".

The tunic was replaced, from 1335, by the Gipon, later called the Doublet, close-fitting, slightly waisted and reaching nearly to the knees; its sleeves were tight, with a row of buttons from the elbow down. The Super-tunic was replaced by the Cotehardie, tight-fitting and buttoned or laced to the waist level, whence it flared into a full skirt open in front to the knees. The hood developed a hanging tail ("Liripipe"), often twisted round the head. The female Kirtle was cut to mould the figure to hip level, the neckline often baring the shoulders. Over it was worn a Cotehardie, close-fitting and low-necked. In addition, the hair, enclosed in a net ("fret") was becoming a conspicuous form of decoration.

It is noticeable that the costume of the peasantry remained ill-adapted to their work, with "skirts" about their knees and head often swathed in a hood even at harvest time. The "new look" did not begin to affect that class until the fifteenth century.

Among the fashionables the second half of the fourteenth century saw the male Gipon (Doublet) becoming shorter and waisted and lavishly ornamented with buttons; the Cotehardie had long flaps ("Tippets") hanging from the elbows. The borders of the garment were often "dagged" (scalloped) and it began to develop a collar. At the end of the fourteenth century long sleeves expanding funnel-wise over the hands came into fashion, the first of that long series of symbolic devices indicating a social class above the manual worker. The leg-hose, of a stretchable material cut on the cross, were often parti-coloured (until 1420) and the shoes (from 1395 to 1410) were "piked", i.e. with long points stuffed out with tow.

An important novelty was the Houppelande (1380 to 1450, when it became known as the Gown). This upper garment fitted the shoulders, but thence fell in deep tubular folds, kept in place by a belt. For ceremonial use it reached the ground, but otherwise was knee-length. It had a high upright collar and the sleeves expanded into an immense funnel shape, the lower edge even reaching the ground. (This garment has survived in the gown of the learned professions.) Borders of garments were lavishly ornamented with dagging (especially from 1380 to 1440), and headgear became very elaborate, with fantastic shapes.

In women's garments, the principal novelty was the Sideless Surcoat (1360 to 1500), developed from the sleeveless surcoat, and now having large side openings from shoulders to hips revealing the close-fitting kirtle

within. This was the first of a long series of such "window" devices designed to attract male notice. The front part of this sideless surcoat formed a stomacher, known as the Plackard. Fashion devoted special attention to the head and hair with a variety of head-dresses, and eyebrow plucking and face-painting were noticeable features (from 1370 to 1480).

In the fifteenth century the male Cotehardie (or Jacket) was shortened, while the Houppelande, long or short, with its huge pendulous sleeves was a conspicuous garment, often elaborately trimmed with costly furs. The hose, the long legs reaching the fork and there joined together to cover the seat, now resembled "tights". The front flap at the fork protruded as a small pouch—the Codpiece (from 1408 to 1575).

A characteristic of the first half of the fifteenth century was the "bowl crop", the hair being cut to resemble a shallow inverted bowl. A large variety of hats, mostly big with wide brims, drew attention to the male head. A similar emphasis was to be seen in women's headgear, chiefly expanding laterally in many forms aided by padding and wiring.

As the fifteenth century advanced the male jacket (becoming after 1500 the Jerkin) acquired shoulder pads ("mahoitres") over which the sleeves were gathered to the shoulder seams, giving a virile breadth and squareness to the male shoulders (a device to enhance the "manly look", which is still employed today). The padded doublet, waisted and short, barely covered the hips. The gown (formerly "houppelande") reaching to the ground or to the knee, retained its tubular folds and full sleeves and often a flat square-cut collar at the back. At the close of the century the toe of the shoe began to acquire a duckbill shape.

The woman's gown, worn over the kirtle, was now (1450 to '80's) being cut with a low neck and moulded to the figure down to the hips; thence flowing into a huge trained skirt hung in folds. A seam at the waist appeared c. 1470, but the gown was still in one piece, often of heavy material, up to 45 feet round the hem. The pinched-in waist was surrounded by an ornamental belt.

A great variety of head-dresses was conspicuous during the second half of the fifteenth century. They were usually tall and tilted back, a truncated cone being the English modification of the French "hennin" or "Steeple head-dress". A notable variety was a large gauze veil supported on a wire frame in the shape of a butterfly with half-spread wings (1450 to 1495). Another was the hood-like surround to the face over an undercap.

Pictures of the late fourteenth and fifteenth centuries reveal all manner of experiments in the art of sex appeal in costume by both men and women, some of which have proved acceptable to later generations. We can also detect fashions obviously designed to emphasize superior social rank by being such that it would be impossible to do manual work in them. Of this, what better symbol than a skirt 45 feet round?

4 *above*. Three kings in short tunics and leg bandages, loosely tied. Cloaks fastened on right shoulders. *St. Aethelwold's Benediction, British Museum.*

5 *left*. Woman in long tunic; long head-veil; shoes. *St. Aethelwold's Benediction, 10th-Century, British Museum.*

above. Men in short tunics, cloaks fastened on right shoulders. Shoes and ckered hose (stockings). St. Stephen in long tunic with girdle over which is a draped mantle. *St. Aethelwold's Benediction, British Museum.*

right. Three women in embroidered tunics and long head-veils. *St. Aethelwold's Benediction, British Museum.*

8. Men in short tunics with girdl
The third tunic is embroidered a
has side vents. 1 and 3. *Cotton M
Claudius B IV, British Museum.*
*Junius XI MS., 11th-Century, Bodle
Library, Oxford.*

9. Women in long enveloping veils and one in a very long-sleeved winter super-tunic. *Cotton MS., Claudius BIV, 11th-Century, British Museum.*

10. Embroidered super-tunic caught up by girdle, showing kirtle, i.e. the body garment worn next the smock. Over thi draped mantle; on the head a swathed veil or coverchief. *Augsb Missal. Harl. MS. 2908, 10th–11th-Century, British Muse*

above. Flight into Egypt; Mary in tunic
kirtle and embroidered super-tunic,
~~mtle~~ and veil. Joseph in large stalked hat.
~~h~~ men in cloaks, short stockings and high
~~es~~. *Gough MS. liturg 2, 12th-Century,
Bodleian Library, Oxford.*

top right. Two women in super-tunics
~~n~~ sleeves having long pendant cuffs, a
~~ure~~ of the twelfth century. The figure on
~~right~~ has two long tresses encased in silk
~~aths~~ called "fouriaux", a fashion indica-
~~of~~ high rank from *c*. 1120 to 1150. *Cotton
MS. Nero CIV, British Museum.*

~~right~~. Three women, the two first swathed
~~mantles~~ and veils; the third in a wide-
~~ved~~ super-tunic, the tight sleeves of the
~~le~~ emerging. The hair hanging loose and
~~overed~~, indicating a maiden. *Cotton MS.
~~ero~~ CIV, 12th-Century, British Museum.*

quıdam· nobılem mulıerem de ſar

14 *above*. A wedding scene; the bridegroom in a herigaut, a loo
overgarment with hanging sleeves; his bride in a furred mantle ov
a kirtle, and on her head a barbette and fillet worn over a fret
reticulated caul). *13th-Century MS., Hereford Cathedral Libra*

15 *left*. A seated nobleman; his long tunic now also called a "cot
with a front vent to the skirt. Stalked cap. Criss-cross leg bandag
(a sign of rank) over soled hose. Long embroidered gloves. *Arch.*
13th-Century, Bodleian Library, Oxford.

16 *above*. Men in a boat; wearing tunics. *Drawings of Matthew Pa
MS. 16, Corpus Christi College, Cambridge.*

17 *centre left*. Offa in a long
"cote", with girdle and thir-
teenth-century sleeves.
*Drawings of Matthew Paris,
Cotton MS., Nero DI, British
Museum.*
Early Thirteenth Century
18 *bottom left*. King Lear and
daughters, the latter in long
trained kirtles with girdles.
*Drawings of Matthew Paris,
MS. 26, Corpus Christi College, Cambridge.*
19 *bottom right*. Peasant
in tunic, long hose (stockings) with garters below the
knees; coif on the head.
*Drawings of Matthew Paris,
MS. 16, Corpus Christi College, Cambridge.*

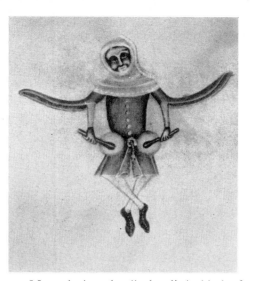

A Saint with staff; wearing a long
[cote]hardie showing buttoned gipon sleeves;
[ ]-lined mantle and decorated shoes.
Luttrell Psalter, 1340, British Museum.

21. Man playing the "nakers" (a kind of
kettle-drum). Wearing a buttoned and
belted cotehardie, an overgarment; the
elbow sleeves with long tippets; decorated
hood and shoes. *The Luttrell Psalter,
British Museum.*

22. Man on horseback hawking. He wears
a cotehardie, hood with liripipe, spurred
boots, and hawking glove. A tabor and
curved drumstick hang from the girdle.
The Luttrell Psalter, British Museum.

23 *left.* Hair-dressing. The lady and her
maid in trained kirtles; the lady having a
plait coiled at the side of her face, and
inspecting it in a mirror; the maid wearing a veil or "kerchief". *The Luttrell
Psalter, British Museum.*

24 *right.* A ploughman in a hat worn back-
wards over a hood; peasant's tunic, socks
and shoes; the peasant's gloves often having one slot for the thumb and two for the
rest of the fingers. The man with a whip
wears a garnache with tongued lapels over
his tunic. *The Luttrell Psalter, British
Museum.*

[ ] Huntsmen wearing a large hat over a
[hoo]d; a garnache with cape-like sleeves
[and] tongue-shaped lapels. Large loose
[boo]ts. *The Luttrel Psalter, British Museum.*

26. Tunic with skirt slit in front; garter on
right stocking ("hose"), the left hitched up
to a button. *The Luttrell Psalter, British
Museum.*

27. Peasant in a cornfield; wearing a tunic
with a front vent and hitched up by the
girdle. On his head a coif. *Holkham MS.
Early 14th-Century, British Museum.*

28 *left*. Putting on a cotehardie over the head; the peasant form of this garment often had no fastenings. *The Luttrell Psalter, British Museum.*

29 *right*. Men with hammock. Peasants in tunics (now sometimes called gipons) with front slit to the skirt and long tight buttoned sleeves. Hoods with "goles" (the cape portion of the hood) and long liripipes (the long pendant tails). *The Luttrell Psalter, British Museum.*

30 *left*. Travelling Family. Women in kirtles; the baby swaddled. Men in garnaches, overgarments with cape-like sleeves falling from the shoulders. *Queen Mary's Psalter, 1320, British Museum.*

31 *right*. Family meeting a bishop. The woman and child in long kirtles and hoods thrown back. Bearded man in hat and garnache, the other man in coif and super-tunic with fitchet (a placket hole for reaching the purse slung from the girdle). *Queen Mary's Psalter, British Museum.*

32 *above*. Serving the meal. The cook cutting up the pig wears a chaperon (originally a hood but now converted into a form of cap). The serving men have removed their aprons. *The Luttrell Psalter, British Museum.*

34 *below*. Stacking corn; peasants in tunics, one with hood and liripipe. All have five-fingered gloves. *The Luttrell Psalter, British Museum.*

33 *above*. Sir Geoffrey Luttrell, wife and guests at table. His wi (on his right) wears a sideless surcote; Sir Geoffrey in a chaperor and tunic with long tight sleeves. The man on his left and the lad on extreme right of picture are wearing cotehardies with elbo sleeve which had long pendant tongues called "tippets". The cu bearer wears a long cotehardie with short tippets. A cloth is drape round his neck. *The Luttrell Psalter, British Museum.*

35 *left*. Joseph a Mary asking for shelt The women wear e broidered aprons; serving maid with ho thrown off. Hair st with bosses covered caul or "fret" (a trellis-work coif skull cap commo worn by unmarr girls). *Holkham M 666, early 14th-Cent British Museum.*

36 *left*. Two women, the one on the right in garde-corps or herigaut, an overgarment generally for winter wear; long hanging sleeves. *Pepysian MS., Magdalene College, Cambridge.*

Early fourteenth century.

37 *right*. Three women in long flowing sleeved surcotes over tight sleeved kirtles; wearing long veils. *Pepysian MS., Magdalene College, Cambridge.*

1382–84.

38 *left*. John Gower, wearing a houppelande. Large hat with bowl-shaped crown and close up-turned brim, worn over a hood. Large loose boots. *Cotton MS., Tiberius A IV, British Museum.*

Fourteenth Century. Second Half.

39 *right*. Three women and an old man, seated. The women in close-fitting kirtles or gowns, waisted. *Pepysian MS., Magdalene College, Cambridge.*

Fifteenth Century.

40 *left*. *c.* 1400. Brass of Civilian and Lady. Man and wife wearing long houppelandes with "bagpipe" sleeves, long undersleeves emerging. This style has high "bottle necks". The man has the gole (cape) of his hood turned down over the high neck. Note his strapped shoes. *Tilbrook Church, Beds.*

41 *right*. 1403. Brass. The women in sideless surcotes and hair arranged in vertical plaits on each side of the face, secured by a fillet crossing the forehead with side pieces. Veils draped behind. *Dartmouth Church, Devon.*

42 *top left. c.* 1415. King Henry V in long ceremonial houppelande w very wide sleeves lined with fur. Doublet sleeves just showing, also n of doublet above the round neck of his houppelande. Occleve in a l houppelande with high bottle neck and bagpipe sleeves. Hair sty "bowl crop" (modern term), fashionable from 1410 to 1460 (but seer tombs as late as 1480). *Arundel MS. 38, British Museum.*

43 *top centre.* 1479–87. The man with arm raised is wearing a very sh doublet laced across a stomacher in front; slashed sleeves laced across shirt sleeves. Long hose; codpiece at the fork. At this date stocki and trunks were in one. Round bonnet. *Eton Chapel Wall Paint*

44 *top right.* 1433. The Birth of St. Edmund. The women in figure-fitt gowns and horned- or heart-shaped head-dresses; one wears a turb *Lydgate's Life of St. Edmund, Harl. MS. 2278, British Museum.*

45 *left.* Early fifteenth century women riders. The one on the left o side saddle; the Wife of Bath astride, and wearing under her large h a goffered veil, a fashion from 1350 to 1420. *Ellesmere Chau*

46. 1446. Brass. Fur-lined ceremonial mantle with heraldic motif worn over a sideless surcote trimmed with fur. Coronet and large "templers" draped with a small veil. *Enfield Church, Middlesex.*

47. *c.* 1410–30. Carving. One shepherd is in a hat worn over a hood and a houppelande with bagpipe sleeves. The man playing the pipe has a "bowl crop" hair style. The others are wearing hoods with deep goles (capes). *Exeter Cathedral.*

48. *c.* 1472. The tinker, in countryn clothes; round hat and hood. B jacket, long hose, and high s with rounded toes. At this date fash able shoes were "piked". *Swaf Church, Norfolk.*

49 *top left*. 1470–80. Edward IV and Richard, Duke of Gloucester. The men on the left and right are in long gowns and bowl hats with rolled brims. The second man on the left is in a short jacket with hanging sleeves, the doublet sleeves emerging. Long hose. All have piked shoes. The kneeling figure in a long gown and chaperon with liripipe suspended from his shoulders. *Royal MS. 15E4, British Museum.*

50 *top right*. 1482. A brass of a lady in a long high-waisted gown with decorated belt. Furred neckline and cuffs. Butterfly head-dress as worn from *c.* 1450 to 1485. *Blickling Church, Norfolk.*

. 1475. Caxton in gown, with hat slung on his der. Man in the background has the fashionable shoes. The ladies in fashionable trained gowns "steeple" head-dresses. The hennin rising to a was a French style. *The Master of Mary of Burgundy.*

52. 1460–80. The Queen and attendant in sideless surcotes with decorated plackards (or stomachers). The three ladies in gowns. Heart-shaped head-dresses. *Cotton MS. Nero. DVII, British Museum.*

53 *above.* 1496. Prince Arthur in a large hat, low-necked doublet and gown. Prince Henry (aged five) dressed as a girl; Princess Margaret in a kirtle, a low hood with decorative border and pendant folds behind and an under-cap or coif. *Engraving of Children of Henry VII, Victoria and Albert Museum.*

54 *left. c.* 1420. Medea and Jason. Both in houppelandes, Medea wearing a heart-shaped head-dress; Jason in a large hat with upturned crown. Attendant has a "bowl crop". *Lydgate's "Sege of Troye", Ryland's Library, Manchester.*

55 *right.* Late fifteenth century. Elizabeth Woodville in a roll head-dress with a V dip over the forehead; her daughters in Turkey hats or bonnets. Their gowns are very *décolleté*, worn with stomachers. *Church window, Little Malvern.*

PART TWO

The Sixteenth Century

Throughout the sixteenth century fashions of both sexes seem principally concerned to glorify social rank. A new aristocracy and a mass of new textiles and costly imports—their use restricted by sumptuary laws to the upper classes—combined to produce new standards of luxury. Fashions were becoming European rather than national. If size is a measure of importance it was male costume which dominated the first half of the century and female costume the second, just as the European scene was overshadowed by male sovereigns in the former and by female sovereigns in the latter.

In the first half of the century male costume comprised a close-fitting quilted Doublet above the top of which the shirt-band was visible, becoming by 1530 a standing collar with frilled edge and commonly embroidered. From that date the doublet always had a skirt, often ribbed, and wide sleeves, commonly detachable. The hose was tied by "points" (ties) through eyelet holes in the doublet, over which was worn a waisted Jerkin having a full skirt, with or without sleeves usually full to the elbow hanging.

The Waistcoat was a short under-doublet, usually quilted. The Gown, worn over doublet and jerkin, was broad-shouldered and hung in heavy folds nearly to the ground. It had a flat collar. A loose buttoned Jacket or "Cassock" was occasionally worn. "Hose" consisted of breeches and stockings ("nether stocks") in one. Surface garments were lavishly decorated with slashings, revealing the coloured linings. Shoes, flat-heeled, were remarkably square-toed, with slashed uppers. Hats, worn indoors as well as out, were large, flat-crowned, and usually plumed. Bonnets and caps, wide and flat, added to the appearance of breadth.

The general effect of such a costume was to enhance the massive burliness of the upper half, even to rendering it top-heavy. However impressive, it lacked any trace of elegance.

The female costume in that half-century comprised gown and kirtle, the former voluminous, moulding the figure to a high waist, and then expanding in heavy folds over the hips to descend to the ground in an ample train. The sleeves opened wide at the wrist, where they were turned back into a gaping cuff. The gown, cut in one piece and lined, had a square-cut neck opening and there was usually a waist-belt or girdle. The kirtle, hidden by the gown, was a front-fastening frock, with a full skirt and sleeves and under-sleeves. Beneath the kirtle was the body garment or Shift, of which the embroidered or laced edge emerged at the neck and wrists.

From 1525 the neckline of the kirtle was low and filled in by a Partlet having a stand-up collar and made of rich material. The skirt of the Kirtle, full-gathered and trained

56. 1530–40's. The Duke of Albany in a flat cap and furred gown with puffed shoulder sleeves, the doublet sleeves emerging. Queen Margaret Tudor wearing a "lettice cap" of fur, the shape fashionable 1500–80 but commonest between 1520 and 1540. Standing collar at the neck and a neckerchief round her shoulders. The style of gown with V neck fashionable 1530 to 1540's. *Painting by Joos van Cleeve.*

until 1530, then became gored to expand in a funnel-shape. A pyramidal front-opening exposed a decorative under-petticoat. A cloak in the shape of a large mantle was occasionally worn.

The head-dress covered an under-cap. A hood, plain or draped, or the "English Hood" (otherwise the Gable or Pediment head-dress) with a pointed arch framing the face, belong to the first quarter of the century. From 1525 the English Hood had its front lappets turned up and the curtain behind replaced by two broad hanging flaps which might be turned up on to the crown of the head. The French Hood (1530 to 1580) was small on a stiff frame and worn far back, exposing the front hair, which was worn smooth with a centre parting. The Bongrace (1530 to 1615) was the curtain of this hood turned forward to lie flat on the crown of the head and projecting beyond the forehead, or it might be a separate piece of stiffened velvet; its purpose was to shield the face from the sun.

The Lettice Cap, of a fur resembling ermine, covered the ears with its side-pieces, while the Caul was a close-fitting cap usually reticulated with gold thread and decorated with jewels. The Coif was a simple linen cap, usually tied under the chin and worn indoors. The Frontlet was an ornamental band worn across the forehead. Costly head ornaments ("Billiments") of precious metals and jewels formed a decorative border to the front of the French hood. While men used slashing, women used embroidery to emphasize the richness of the costume.

In the second half of the century it was said (Nashe, 1593) that men "shew the swelling of their mind in the swellings and plumping out of their apparel" ("Christs teares over Jerusalem", 1593), the doublet and trunk hose being immensely padded ("bombasted"), while the fop prided himself on a waist pinched in by tight lacing. The body of the doublet was also stiffened with buckram, and from 1575 to 1600 the point at the waist in front was so padded as to bulge forward (the "Peascod belly"). Its skirt was shortened and the high collar often tabbed ("pickadils"). Sleeves headed by wings over the shoulder-seams were usually full and often detachable. The jerkin was generally sleeveless. The trunk-hose might be continuous with the stockings ("whole hose") or have thigh-fitting extensions to the knees, known as "canions" over which the stockings were pulled.

Knee-breeches were introduced in 1570, and whether tight or loose were known as "Venetians". The cloak was extremely fashionable, circular or flaring from the shoulders. The Mandilion was a loose jacket, hip-length, with hanging sleeves, and the modish habit was to wear it awry or "Colley-westernwards". The Cassock was a loose jacket with full sleeves.

The neckwear comprised at first a turned-down collar ("falling band") attached to the top of the shirt. By 1560 its frilled edge had developed into a Ruff, which soon became a large separate article tied on by strings. The huger forms (e.g. the "cartwheel ruff" of 1580) were supported on wire frames, the ruff itself stiffened with starch.

Shoes with rounded toes and high riding boots with turnover tops were now fashionable. Flat heels continued. Headgear, rather low and flat to 1570, then shot upwards, a fashionable shape being the sugar-loaf or Copotain hat with high conical crown, "sometimes standyng a quarter of a yarde above the crowne of their heads . . . as please the fantasies of their wavering mindes" (P. Stubbes: *Anatomie of Abuses*, 1583).

Immense attention was paid by the Exquisite to his hair and beard, scented, oiled and curled, with a lovelock gracefully falling on to the chest, and the face artfully coloured.

Female dress in that second half-century introduced the novelty of bodice and skirt as separate garments, allowing unrestricted expansion of the latter. The bodice, tight-fitting, had a short point at the waist, the neck high or low, the sleeves ceasing (1560) to be funnel-shaped and becoming close-fitting, commonly with a puffing at the shoulder. From 1580 the front of the bodice was filled in with a stiff stomacher, the neckline low and the sleeves in the "leg of mutton" shape, known as cannon or trunk sleeves. The separate skirt, now called the Kirtle, was supported on a hooped frame, the Farthingale. The Spanish type (from 1545) was pyramidal or domed, often open in front, to expose an ornamental panel, and for ceremonial use slightly trained.

From 1560 the Spanish was replaced by the French farthingale, tub-shaped, under which a padded bolster (the "bum-roll") was tied round the waist. In 1580 this developed into the "wheel farthingale" as though the were a horizontal wheel round the waist over which t skirt was stretched for some four feet, then falli vertically over the edge, which in 1590 was given a frill border. The whole costume presented the apotheosis immobility, with every joint in the body rigidly co strained. Nevertheless, ladies danced in it, and, we a told, Queen Elizabeth danced "higher" than her riv Mary of Scotland.

An additional garment for warmth or ceremony w the Gown worn over the bodice and skirt; this was som times loose-bodied, sometimes close-fitting. Its sleeve when present, were short and puffed. The garmer reaching the ground, was usually worn open, sometim with a narrow sash at the waist.

The principal neckwear was the conspicuous Ruff various forms, the larger ones wired. Unlike the male ru this, in women, might be open in front. The vast Car wheel ruff (1580 to 1610) and its smaller versions we worn with high or low-necked bodices, while the Fan shaped ruff (1570 to 1625) was worn—with a low-nec by the unmarried—the ruff rising up from the sides an back of the *décolletage* to spread out fanwise at the bac of the head. A huge wired Head Rail (1590 to 162 formed an arch over the head and was worn chiefly b widows. At the wrists hand-ruffs or turned-back cuffs lawn or lace were additional impedimenta of rank.

Headgear comprised hoods, bonnets, hats and cap Hoods, developing from the French hood, tended increase in size, while the Marie-Stuart hood (which v associate with that queen) was a small hood of law edged with lace and its front border dipping over th forehead.

Hats and bonnets, often indistinguishable from eac other, were mostly worn for travelling or for riding; the were inclined to be flat, with a plume, and worn tilted one side. "English burgher women usually wear hig hats covered with velvet or silk" (Platter's *Travels England*, 1599). Indoor caps and reticulated cauls resemb ing hair-nets were elaborately trimmed, but it was corre for younger women at least to go bare-headed even ou of doors.

The hair was plaited and coiled at the back of the hea the forehead always left uncovered. False hair and actu wigs, together with hair dyes, were in fashion, and at th close of the century patches were beginning to be applie to the face.

Stockings, commonly with embroidered clocks, wei now being knitted. Shoes were without heels. Glove elaborately worked and perfumed, were fashionable, an jewellery was much in use, precious stones being abun dantly attached to the surface of ceremonial garments The upper classes were clothed mainly in silk, leavin woollens for their inferiors. Portraits, of the forme group at least, give an impression of an arrogant tast singularly lacking in aesthetic sensibility. "When you posterity shall see our pictures they shall think wee wei foolishly proud of apparel." (Verstegen's *Antiquitie concerning the English Nation*, 1605.)

57 *left*. 1513. James IV in a gown with hanging sleeves, the doublet sleeves emerging; long hair and small "bonnet" with close upturned brim absent in front.

58 *right*. Margaret Tudor in a fitting gown and English hood with small forehead rolls concealing the hair. *Municipal Library, Arras.*

op *right*. 1517. Male figure wearing doublet with low square neck showing the neck of the shirt e it. Gown with wide sleeves. Shoes with broad toes, low uppers and instep strap. *Tong Church, Staffs.*

nd 61 *bottom left and centre*. 1507. Brass of a man in a long gown edged with fur; wide sleeves; e suspended from his girdle. Shoes with broad toes and very low uppers. Hair worn long to cover the neck. His wife in gown and English hood. *Great Cressingham Church, Norfolk.*

ottom *right*. 1501. Elizabeth of York wearing the early form of English hood with wired-up, pointed some hair being visible. Folds of material fall behind, a decorative border frames the face and long lled lappets crossing the head fall low on each side. A white under-cap was usual. *National Portrait Gallery.*

ELIZABETHA VXOR
HENRICI VII

63. *c.* 1548. "Young Man in Red"; his doublet worn open to show the black work embroidery on his shirt, repeated on the sleeve frills at the wrists. Short gown. Upper stocks (i.e. breeches portion) paned and continued as nether stocks (the stocking portion) but forming one garment. Codpiece. Narrow belt for dagger and sword. Shoes of a new fashion, rounded toes and closed up to the ankles. Flat cap. *G. Stretes, Hampton Court.*

64. *c.* 1545. Prince Edward, later King Edward VI, i doublet buttoned down the front; over it a fur-trimmed g with hanging sleeves. Flat cap and feather. Shoes slashed covering the feet up to the ankles, a new style starting the 1540's and contrasting with the previous mode (from 1 when the uppers were often merely toe-caps. *Audley I Essex.*

65 *left.* The Bead-Teller. 1543. He wears a plain doublet with belt hung with a purse and dagger. Hose consists of upper stocks (later puffed out and called "trunk hose") and nether stocks, the two joined forming one garment. He wears a "flat cap" and hair to the nape of the neck, a fashion which went out among the upper classes in the 1530's. *From tomb of Nicholas Purefoy at Fenny Drayton.*

66 *right. c.* 1544. Henry VIII in a slashed, long-skirted doublet under a gown with puffed elbow-sleeves, the doublet sleeves emerging. Prominent codpiece. Flat cap and feather. Strapped shoes with broad scanty uppers (a type known as "voided shoes"), a style just going out of fashion. Prince Edward is similarly dressed. Queen Catherine Parr wears an English hood and trained gown open to show the petticoat which was part of the dress. *Hampton Court.*

bove. 1520's. Catherine of Aragon in an English hood of later (1520's–1540). Side lappets turned up and striped rolls under **o**inted arch concealing the hair. The curtain behind was now **w**o broad strips of material. Low square-necked gown with decorative under-sleeves. *National Portrait Gallery*.

p right. c. 1530. Anne Boleyn wearing a small French hood far **o**n the head exposing the hair and ornamented with two rows **w**els known as "upper and nether billiments". The pendant **b**ehind was in one piece, narrow and straight. *National Portrait Gallery*.

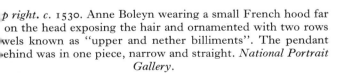

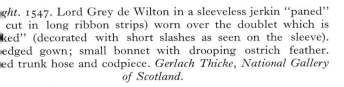

ght. 1547. Lord Grey de Wilton in a sleeveless jerkin "paned" **c**ut in long ribbon strips) worn over the doublet which is **k**ed" (decorated with short slashes as seen on the sleeve). **e**dged gown; small bonnet with drooping ostrich feather. **ed** trunk hose and codpiece. *Gerlach Thicke, National Gallery of Scotland*.

70 *left. c.* 1550. Lady Cornwallis in a close-bodied gown and closed ruff; is wearing a French hood with the pendant flap turned up over the head and in this position known as a "bongrace"; supposed to shade the eyes. She holds a pomander containing a perfumed mixture thought to protect against infection. *Audley End, Essex.*

71 *right.* 1559. Queen Elizabeth in a loose gown worn for warmth over ordinary dress, the sleeves of which are visible. She holds a pair of gloves. *Engraving by Finck.*

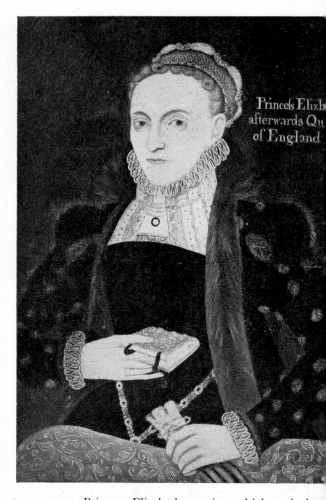

72. 1550. Sir Thomas Gresham in a buff jerkin with stand collar and short sleeves, worn over a doublet. Both are decorated with short slashes generally called "pinking".

73. *c.* 1555. Princess Elizabeth wearing a high-necked pa covering a *décolletage.* Small ruff and hand-ruff. Fur-e gown.

1567. Ann, daughter of Sir William Brown, in a [clos]e-bodied gown, high collar and ruff. Note the [watc]h suspended from a ribbon round the neck, a [very] unusual feature as watches had not long been invented. *Ingatestone Hall, Essex.*

right. 1562. Duchess of Norfolk in a close-[bod]ied gown with short over-sleeves and sham [han]ging-sleeves, represented by pendant strips. *Audley End, Essex.*

76 *left.* 1569. Man wearing a fur-faced ceremonial gown, flat cap and dark coif. *Audley End, Essex.*

77 *right.* 1569. Lady Elizabeth Audley in a loose over-gown with elbow sleeves and high collar; open ruff. She wears a widow's hood over a white coif, and holds a pair of gloves. *Audley End, Essex.*

78. Monument to Roger Lygon and Katherine his wife, c. 1575 to 1580. The husband, in armour, wearing a slight peascod-bellied doub short trunk hose and small ruff; his wife in a gown with wings and girdle suspending a pomander; small ruff and French hood. *Fair, Church, Glos.*

79 *left*. 1574. James VI of Scotland in a sleeveless jerkin fastened by three breast buttons only; the doublet sleeves emerging. Full pear-shaped breeches ("Venetians") with pickadil border below the knees. Shoes with rounded toes, pinked. Small bonnet with feather and closed ruff. *National Portrait Gallery.*

80 *right*. 1575-6. Queen Elizabeth at a Hunt Picnic. She wears a tall hat with feathers. The men in doublets and bombasted trunk-hose. *Turberville's "Booke of Hunting", British Museum.*

81 *left*. 1565. Lord Darnley, his doublet with the high stand-collar fashionable in the 1560's. Small ruff and hand-ruffs; sleeves with small wings in "pickadil" (tabbed) matching the short skirt of his doublet. Deep paned trunk hose and codpiece. *Lord Bolton.*

82 *right*. 1579. Earl of Leicester in a doublet with a short skirt and slight "peascod belly", fashionable from *c.* 1575 to 1600. Short paned trunk-hose. A furred cassock. At the neck he wears a small turned-down collar ("falling band") instead of a ruff. *University College, Oxford.*

1568. Hugh Fitzwilliam in a pinked sleeveless jerkin wings and high stand collar; small ruff open with dang-"band strings" three a side. Doublet sleeves edged with adils and hand-ruffs. At this date ruffs and hand-ruffs e attached to the shirt. *Sir A. More, The Earl Fitzwilliam.*

84. *c.* 1562. Katherine Countess of Hertford and son. The mother in a fur-edged gown with high-necked partlet and compound ruff; small lawn Marie-Stuart hood. The child in long robes, sleeveless but with "wings" above the under-sleeves and sham hanging sleeves. A large "muckinder" (handkerchief) suspended from the waist and a bib under the chin. Small feathered cap. *Audley End, Essex.*

85. 1578. Sir Edward Hoby in a very tall hat with feather and goldsmithry hatband, very fashionable at the period. Closed embroidered ruff; doublet pinked and slashed. *Miss P. Vansittart-Neale.*

86 *right.* 1575–80. Unknown lady, in a gown with square *décolletage* covered by a partlet. Wings to the bishop sleeves matching the forepart of the under-skirt. Billiment head ornament. *National Portrait Gallery.*

87 *left.* 1568–9. Marriage Fe with town and country fo The gentlemen in double trunk-hose and some with cloa or gowns. The ladies in op robes and small Spanish fa thingales. Peasants in lo coats, the women with neck chiefs and aprons. *Jons Ha nagel, Hatfield House, Hert*

1582. Sir Henry Nevill wearing a [fash]ionable short cassock, fur-lined with [hi]gh collar under the closed ruff; and a [roun]d-crowned soft hat. *Sir Edmund Bacon.*

89. 1586. Sir Henry Unton wearing a large closed ruff, very fashionable 1580–1610, and tall hat with cypress hat-band, also jewel and feather. *E. Peter Jones.*

90. 1589. John Bull wearing a falling band (i.e. turned-down collar) which began to replace the ruff from *c.* 1540. It is embroidered with black work. *Faculty of Music, Oxford.*

91 *left*. 1582. Sir Christopher Hatton wearing a peascod-bellied doublet with very short skirt, trunk-hose and decorative canions over which his stockings are rolled. "Pantofles" (i.e. overshoes) which were sometimes called "mules" in the sixteenth century. A short cloak matching his trunk-hose; he carries a Court bonnet with button hat-band. *Cornelius Ketel, Earl of Winchelsea.*

92 *right*. 1588–90. A youth in doublet with "peascod belly", very short trunk-hose and long nether stocks. Closed ruff; a cloak over one shoulder. *Nicholas Hilliard, Victoria and Albert Museum.*

93 *above*. 1585–87. Brasses. The elder boy in a long coat with a muckinder suspended from his girdle. 94 *top centre*: the younger boy in swaddling clothes. *Merstham Church, Surrey.*

95 *top right*. 1588. Henry Lord Windsor. He wears armour with peascod belly and matching embroidered falling band (i.e. collar) and cuffs. *The Earl of Plymouth.*

96 *below left*. 1588. Lord William Russell in a doublet with "peascod belly". Close-fitting venetians with stockings drawn up over them. *The Duke of Bedford.*

97 *below right*. 1587. Sir William Pelham. Wearing armour with the peascod-belly fashionable at the period; short trunk hose and prominent codpiece; matching ruff and hand-ruffs. *Portrait ascribed to Zucchero, The Earl of Yarborough.*

right. 1590. Family group. A widow with
ow's head-dress; long pointed stomacher
to the bodice, large closed ruff. The hus-
's portrait with ruff; the sons with falling
s. The little girls are dressed like their
er. *Attributed to Franz Pourbus the younger,
Sir William Worsley.*

low centre. 1596. Brass of a woman in a
with stomacher-front and ruff; tight
es; small French farthingale; under the
skirt is an embroidered forepart. On the
is a wired-up arched hood draping the
lders, and a small French hood. *Necton
Church, Norfolk.*

below right. 1596 style. Brass of a widow
608) in a gown over a small French
ingale but without an embroidered forepart. *Felbrigg Church, Norfolk.*

below. 1592. The sisters Fitton wearing
s with pointed stomacher-fronts, bom-
d "cannon" sleeves, frounced skirts over
l farthingales; closed ruffs and hair raised
ads. *From "Gossip from a Muniment
" ed. by Lady Newdigate-Newdegate.*

102 *above left. c.* 1595. Sir John Petre in a doublet with narr[ow] tabbed skirt and close sleeves with wings; trunk-hose witho[ut] codpiece which was discarded in the 1590's. He wears a ruff [and] falling band together, a fashion from *c.* 1580 to 1615. *Ingate[stone] Hall, Essex.*

103 *above.* 1592. Queen Elizabeth in a gown with a frounced [skirt] worn over a large French or wheel farthingale. "Cannon" sle[eves] (also called "trunk sleeves") and large hanging sleeves. She ca[rries] a folded fan and gloves with tabbed cuffs. *National Portrait Gal[lery].*

104 *left.* 1599. Sir Henry Neville in a compound flattened ru[ff,] sleeveless jerkin with wings over a pinked doublet clo[sely] buttoned. *Audley End, Essex.*

PART THREE

The Seventeenth Century

his political century saw a significant breach in social rriers; gentlemen began to wear woollen cloth for their y suits, a material hitherto used only by their inferiors. Male costume in this century presents four phases. To e end of James I's reign (1625) it remained in the bulky zabethan tradition. Under Charles I a slimmer elegance ove to emphasize vertical lines. Although Puritan and valier dress had their characteristics, a drab severity s more a feature of class than of creed. "The leaders d their wives were as well dressed on the one side as the other." ("Memoirs of the Life of Colonel Hutchinn, by his Widow Lucy".) The Restoration (1660) of arles II introduced an extravagance of modes copied m the French Court, but some certainly did not spread beyond Whitehall. By 1680 experiments towards dern construction, with signs of "cut and fit", were ing attempted, thanks to the wider use of woollen th.

The waistline after 1625 was somewhat higher, as the doublet lost its padding and its corset-shape. Its skirt had deep square tabs. By 1640 it shortened to expose the shirt in the gap above the top of the breeches.

The jerkin as a civilian garment was discarded after 1630. The mandilion, known after 1620 as a "Manderville", was a loose thigh-length overcoat. Cloaks, long and short, were much in fashion until 1660. Trunk-hose, much distended and with or without canions, became replaced by knee-breeches, full or close-fitting or open like modern "shorts" and from 1630 long-legged to the calf. The gown had now become a ceremonial garment or used by the elders and the learned professions.

Of neckwear, the Standing Ruff, sewn to a deep neckband in double or treble layers of goffering, survived to c. 1620; the Falling Ruff, dropping downwards, from 1615 to 1640's. The Falling Band (to 1670's) resembled a smooth turned-down collar, sometimes wide across the

05. c. 1600–5. Alderman Isaac Walton and Wife. The wife in a doublet bodice, frounced skirt over a small French farthingale; earing a "Copotain" hat with cable-twist crêpe hat-band and a compound ruff. Her husband in a fur-faced gown with long anging sleeves; short skirted doublet, long trunk-hose with canions covered by stockings with sash garters below the knees. Shoes with ribbon ties. *From their tomb in St. Nicholas Church, Gloucester.*

shoulders or spreading over the top of the chest. The Standing Band ("Golilla") from 1605 to 1630 was a semi-circular collar round the back of the neck.

Boots and shoes acquired heels from 1600, the toes rounded to 1635, and then square and tapering. A striking ornament on the uppers of shoes was a large rosette. Boots with huge cup-shaped tops and "bucket tops" with "butterfly" spur-leathers and spurs were worn for walking as well as for riding. Coloured knitted stockings in silk or wool were secured by conspicuous garters.

Hats were large, with wide brims and a plume as favoured by Cavaliers, the Puritans preferring the old "sugarloaf" shape. The hair was worn long on to the shoulders, often with a lovelock dangling on to the chest, a Cavalier mode condemned by strict Puritans.

Female costume until 1625 was still Elizabethan in style, comprising bodice (low-necked with a stomacher or high-necked without) and skirt, known as the "petticoat". The low *décolletage* might even expose the breasts in the unmarried (but marriage was common at fourteen). The high-necked bodice was fastened down the front and ruffs were worn with both forms. Sleeves were wide above, narrowing to the wrist and finished with a small cuff or hand-ruff. Huge hanging sleeves were often added.

The "wheel farthingale" persisted to 1615 and reduced in size to 1620, giving a tub-shape to the skirt which was short enough to expose the feet. A full-gathered skirt, slightly trained, was beginning to replace the farthingale by 1615. All skirts might be open in front to expose a decorative "forepart" of the under-skirt.

The formal gown was rare after 1620 but a négligée version of it, spoken of as a "nightgown" though worn out of doors, was fashionable.

After 1625 new styles appeared, such as a high-waisted bodice with or without basques, and having ballooned sleeves and a skirt gathered at the waist to fall in full folds to the ground. The skirt was often hitched up all round, or it might have a front opening.

Various forms of ruff and standing bands tended after 1625 to be replaced by a cape-like neckerchief, the Rail. Similarly hand-ruffs gave way to cuffs. Ribbon bows were much used to decorate the front of the corsage. Cloaks were voluminous and Tippets (capes) might be worn as additional garments indoors.

All through the century it was fashionable to be bare-headed out of doors, the former hoods gradually becoming worn only by the elders. Indoor caps ("coifs"), usually white, were commonly worn over the back of the head, concealing the hair coiled there in a "bun". A forehead fringe was a distinctive feature from 1620 to 1645, the side hair hanging in corkscrew curls.

After the Restoration, there was a strong inclination for a "new look", and experiments were made. Charles II himself introduced the Vest and Tunic, supposed to be an Eastern style, the vest flowing loosely to the knees with a loose cloak-like tunic over it; but this was replaced (c. 1668) by a coat somewhat more shaped and reaching to below the knees, receiving from 1680 a closer fit, the sleeves with deep turned-back cuffs, collar; worn over a waistcoat nearly as long, and at t neck a hanging cravat and ruffles at the wrist.

A remarkable form of breeches, with immensely wi legs pleated into a waistband and reaching the knees, w the Rhinegraves or Petticoat-breeches (1660's to 1670 These were lavishly trimmed with loops of coloured ri bons round the waist and legs. The more usual style w closed breeches having wide "bloomer" legs oft flounced at the knee.

Stockings with "stirrup" feet and legs expanding wide above the knees were enriched with decorative fri turned down over the garters and known as Port Cano (1660 to 1670); these were worn only with open breech From 1690 stockings were drawn up over the legs of t breeches and turned down in a flat roll above the kne hence known as "roll-ups" or "rollers", a style employ only by the gentry.

Boots were ceasing to be fashionable except for ridi Of overcoats the fashionable form was the Brandenbu reaching the calf, and replacing the cloak after 16 Hats, gradually ceasing to be worn indoors or in chur were assuming a flat "boater" shape or a low round cro and a broad brim cocked up. The most conspicuous featu of the whole costume was the full-bottomed wig, immens large and descending on to the shoulders, or, for travelli the "Campaign wig", full but shorter.

In women's costume of the second half-century t bodice-and-skirt style continued to 1675 but now lon waisted, some with short tabs flaring out over the hips, t low *décolletage* with a broad lace "whisk" (similar to "bertha"), the sleeves full to the elbow with a wi opening edged with a lace fall, the frilled sleeve of t shift emerging below it. The voluminous skirt w usually open in front, the train lengthening after 1670.

The Gown style, from 1680, with close-fitting bodi attached to a trained skirt open in front, had an und skirt edged with a flounce. The Mantua or Nightgov resembled the gown but was looser and used as a néglig

The neckwear included the Whisk of lace worn acr the top of the off-the-shoulder *décolletage*, the Ste kirk or neck scarf, its ends twisted and pinned aside, a the Pinner or modesty "fill-in" (but the name was al used for a white cap and for the bib of an apron).

The bare-headed fashion persisted, but large hats wi tall crowns and wide brims were also worn together wi hoods. The Fontange (1690 to 1710) was a headdress stiff frills of linen in the shape of a half-open fan standi up on the top of the head and held in place by a wi frame, the Commode. The hair was elaborately dress in curls and ringlets, with an ever-increasing addition false hair building up a tall mass on the head. Elabora facial make-up was the fashionable mode, including t use of patches, false eyebrows and cheek-plumpers.

Muffs and canes were carried by both sexes. Fashio after the Restoration, were much borrowed from Franc and ladies' shoes, with nearly pointed toes, acquired Lo heels.

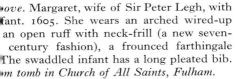

...ove. Margaret, wife of Sir Peter Legh, with
...fant. 1605. She wears an arched wired-up
... an open ruff with neck-frill (a new seven-
...century fashion), a frounced farthingale
... The swaddled infant has a long pleated bib.
...m tomb in Church of All Saints, Fulham.

...p right. 1600–15. Tomb figures. Scarves
... above the fan-shaped ruffs; frounced
...gale skirts; sham hanging sleeves (i.e. flat
...nt bands representing leading strings for
children). *Pershore Abbey, Worcs.*

...ght. c. 1600. Lady Petre in an open fan-
...d ruff with neck-frill, a feature first known
...o. Long-pointed stomacher-front, cannon
...s and frounced skirt over a wheel farthingale.
Ingatestone Hall, Essex.

35

109 *above*. 1605. King James I and Queen. He wears a short-skirted doublet and short breeches open at the knees (sometimes called "slop-hose"). Sash garters; copotain hat. The queen in a tight bodice, skirt without a frounce showing the hard line of the wheel-farthingale within. Open ruff with neck-frill. *Engraving by Jan Wierix.*

110 *above*. 1613. Earl and Countess of Somerset. He we doublet, trunk-hose, French cloak and plumed hat. His in a frounced farthingale skirt, low-necked bodice wi sleeves and hanging sleeves; and a Marie-Stuart head-o *Engraving.*

111 *left*. 1600–10. "Two Kinde Lovers." The man in doublet, trunk-hose with canions, and long boots with spurs; French cloak; large hat with feather. The woman in doublet-bodice, sleeves with wings and sham hanging sleeves. The female "doublet bodice" was fashionable until *c.* 1625 and subsequently worn for riding. She has a full skirt but no farthingale. Hair wired up. *Woodcut, Roxburghe Ballads.*

112 *left*. 1610–15. Crude woodcut of the period, the man in round hose, doublet and French cloak. Husband and wife wear semi-circular standing bands (style fashionable 1605 to 1630). The wife in a Marie-Stuart hood. The boys in Dutch breeches or long slop-hose. *Roxburghe Ballads.*

113 *above*. Early seventeenth century. Queen in a frounced skirt over a wheel farthingal open in front revealing an elegant petticoat. sleeves with sham hanging sleeves. Deep sta band (collar) and hair wired up and decorated jewels. *Engraving by R. Elstracke, British Mu*

114 *left*. 1615–20. Lady Dorothy Carey in an embroidered jacket (also called a "waistcoat") and full embroidered skirt. No farthingale. The overgown with hanging sleeves. Shoes with large "shoe-roses" (rosettes). Semicircular standing band and on her head a cap known as a "shadow". *Peterborough Museum*.

115 *right*. 1611. John Florio in a sleeveless fur-edged gown (as now worn by the learned professions) over his doublet; compound ruff in flattened convolutions (style fashionable from *c*. 1585 to 1620). *From MS. Dictionary*.

above. 1617. Men in tight doublets, full trunk-hose. *Title page of "A Faire Quarrell" by Middleton and Rowley*.

117 *above*. Lady Isabella Rich 1615–20. Dressed similarly to Lady Dorothy Carey (114) but with drapery instead of an overgown and the jacket is cut with extreme *décolletage*—the mode for unmarried women—even to exposing the breasts, from *c*. 1605 to 1625. *Peterborough Museum*.

118. 1620. The Daughters of Lord Teynham. They wear gowns without farthingales; note the sham hanging sleeves as then worn by young women and stand-fall or falling ruffs. The daughter on the extreme left shows the excessive *décolletage* denoting an unmarried girl. *Sepulchral Effigy, Lynsted Church, Kent.*

119. 1616. Earl of Dorset in a short-skirted doublet, tight sle with wings; a military gorget under a semi-circular standing b Full short trunk-hose continued as nether stocks with embroid clocks. Large shoe "roses". *Miniature by Isaac Oliver, Victoria Albert Museum.*

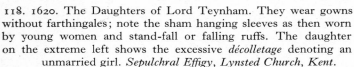

120 *left*. Robert Carr, Earl of Somerset. Portrait attritubed to John Hoskins, *c.* 1620–5. Wearing a falling ruff and the fashionable Roman T or "Hammer" cut beard. The moustache forms the cross-piece of the T or hammer. *National Portrait Gallery.*

121 *right*. 1612. A boy twelve months old, dressed like a girl in frounced skirt, tight bodice and coif, standing band, and cuffs edged with matching lace.
(N.B. Until near the end of the eighteenth century boys were dressed like girls up to the age of six or seven when they were "breeched", i.e. dressed like men.) *The Hon. Andrew Shirley.*

122. 1620–5. Margaret Laton in an embroidered jacket and apron; deep lace falling ruff. On her head a cap known as a "shadow" or "cornet". *Lord Rothermere*.

123. *c.* 1625. Duke of Buckingham in a doublet dipping to a sharp point with tabbed skirts; sleeves with wings and the upper portion as well as the trunk-hose paned. Long hose, no canions, ceremonial style at this date. Large shoe-roses. *Painting by D. Mytens, The Earl Fitzwilliam.*

124. 1625. Sir H. Vere in a sleeveless winged jerkin with sh hanging sleeves, worn over a doublet. Cloak-bag breeches trimr below with points (ribbon) tipped with aglets (metal tags). Th breeches were very fashionable in the 1620's and 1630's. A s shoulder-belt for his sword. Boots show the fashionable wrinkli "One that more admires the good wrinkle of a boot". (1606. "Ret from Parnassus".) *Painting by Cornelius Jansen, Christchu Mansion, Ipswich.*

125 *left. c.* 1620. Woodcut. "The Merry Hostess". The ma doublet, "cloak-bag breeches" trimmed above the knees v ribbon loops; sash garters. Shoe-roses. The woman ii stomacher-fronted gown and tabbed bodice; large apron broad handkerchief or "rail" and Marie-Stuart cap. *Roxbu Ballads.*

above. 1620–5. The man is in a doublet, Venetians, cloak and large
The woman wears a similar hat, a falling ruff, a gown cut low
gh to expose the breasts (a fashion among the unmarried from
05 to 1625). She also wears a "safeguard" (a skirt or half-skirt to
protect her clothes from dirt). *Contemporary woodcut.*

right. 1621. Man in a doublet with tabbed skirts descending to a
t in front; sleeves with wings; short "cloak-bag" (oval) breeches
out the usual ribbon trimmings. Sash garters. Falling ruff; broad-
med hat. *Title page of Burton's "Anatomy of Melancholy".*

1628. Duke of Buckingham and Family. He wears a matching doublet and breeches. His wife in the new-fashion gown with double
ooned and slashed sleeves, sometimes called "virago" sleeves. On her head a shadow or cornet. The daughter is similarly dressed.
baby in a coif, long gown with leading strings and a ribbon suspending a coral (worn as a protection against witchcraft). *Painting by
G. Houthorst, National Portrait Gallery.*

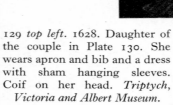

129 *top left*. 1628. Daughter of the couple in Plate 130. She wears apron and bib and a dress with sham hanging sleeves. Coif on her head. *Triptych, Victoria and Albert Museum.*

130 *top right*. 1628. Husband and wife; he wears a gown over his doublet and holds fringed gloves. Both wear closed falling ruffs and spreading cuffs. The wife has a frill at the neck, a seventeenth century feature when a ruff was worn. Note her large hat. *Triptych, Victoria and Albert Museum.*

131 *left*. 1628. Son of the couple in Plate 130, in a doublet with sham hanging sleeves and wearing a long skirt; large hat and fringed gloves. *Triptych, Victoria and Albert Museum.*

132 *above*. 1620. Two ladies in frounced skirts over French farthingales which by 1620 were going out of fas Tight bodices; one with a round waist known as a "I waist". Closed ruffs. Hair raised on pads. *Detail fro Misses Griffiths by Marc Geerharts, Marcus Wic Boynton, Esq.*

1630. Boy aged five in a doublet like
[m]an's worn with a long "petticoat"
[a]s used for a skirt) open in front to
[show] the under-petticoat. Lace-edged
[long] band and cuffs. Broad hat. *Christchurch Mansion, Ipswich.*

134. 1632. Boy aged six in a male doublet
with sham hanging sleeves used as leading
strings. Long petticoat. Broad falling band, a
shape typical of the 1630's. Coif on the head.
A large muckinder (handkerchief) suspended from the girdle. *Ingatestone Hall, Essex.*

135. *c.* 1638. Princess Mary, daughter of
Charles I, in a low-necked gown and
decorative apron; hair in the fashionable
style. *Portrait by Sir A. Vandyke, Normanton collection.*

c. 1630. Dame Elizabeth Pettus in a dress with basqued
[bod]ice and stomacher-front. The sleeves slashed and joined
[by] ribbon bows; lace-edged neckerchief and shadow or
cornet on the head. *Norwich Castle Museum.*

137. 1635. A Lady showing the typical hair style of 1635–45.
She wears double puffed and paned "virago sleeves".

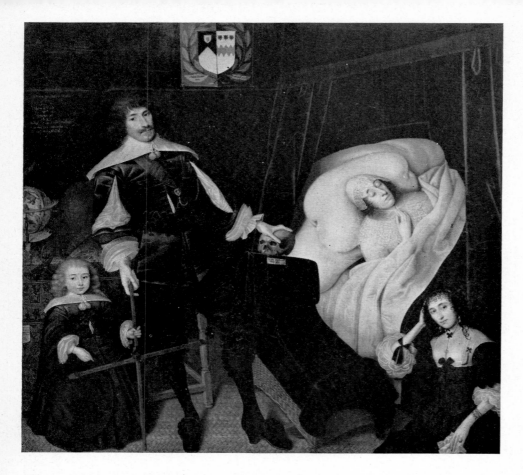

138 *left.* 1635. Death-bed scene.
husband and children in mourn
He has decorative points at the w
and knees of his breeches. Father
son have very wide falling bands
large tasselled band-strings. The
boy is in petticoats, holding
father's hat. The daughter in
fashionable hair-style and block b
*Sir Thomas Aston at the death
of his wife, by John Souch, Manch.
City Art Gallery.*

139. *c.* 1639. Two young men in loose short-waisted doublets, Spanish hose, lace boot-hose tops and clogs. *Lords John and Bernard Stuart by Sir A. Vandyke, Countess Mountbatten of Burma.*

140. 1631. Charles I in a doublet with breast and sleeves paned; cloak-bag breeches, boots wrinkled, known as a "quail-pipe boot". Butterfly spur leathers and fringed gauntlet gloves. *Painting by Daniel Mytens, National Portrait Gallery.*

141. 1638. Lady in a basqued bod "chaperone" hood and carries a m *Hollar's "Ornatus Muliebris".*

142 *left*. 1634. Sir Daniel Goodricht in a leather jerkin with stuff sleeves or wings only with the doublet sleeves emerging. The slit in the sleeves was often used as a pocket for the handkerchief. A lace-edged falling band over a military gorget. *Painting attributed to A. van Hult, City of York Art Gallery.*

143. 1635. George Wither in a fashionable wide falling band and tasselled band-strings. Broad-brimmed hat; bodkin beard and waxed moustache. *Contemporary Engraving.*

144 *below*. 1635–40. The husband in a loose short-waisted doublet. Sash garters and high-heeled shoes with ribbon shoe-strings. Long hair and sugar-loaf hat previously called a "Copotain". The little girls are dressed as adults; the baby in a baby's mantle. *The Saltonstall Family, by David des Granges, Sir Kenneth Clark.*

145 *left*. 1639. Lady showing the fashionable hair style. She carries a muff and a stole (sometimes known as a "flea-fur"). *Hollar's "Ornatus Muliebris"*.

146 *right*. 1639. A lady in a full long overcoat ("cassock") and a hood (known as a "chaperone") and a half-mask ("loo mask") with muff and feather fan with mirror. *Hollar's "Ornatus Muliebris"*.

147. 1639. A lady in a basqued bodice with very low *décolletage*. Puffed elbow sleeves and long gloves. Very fashionable hair-style. *Hollar's "Ornatus Muliebris"*.

148. 1640. Countrywoman carrying a shopping-basket; she wears a plain coif, neckerchief, and shows an under-petticoat. Her shoes are raised on pattens. *Hollar's "Ornatus Muliebris"*.

149. 1639–40. Countrywoman wearing apron, "gorget" covering *décolletage*, and closed oval ruff worn only in the seventeenth cent *Hollar's "Ornatus Muliebris"*

150 *left*. 1640. Lady wearing the fashionable gauze veil head-dress; with neckerchief and long gloves. *Hollar's "Ornatus Muliebris"*.

151 *right*. 1640. Lady wearing a loo-mask, large neckerchief and muff. The skirt is hitched up to show the decorative petticoat. *Hollar's "Ornatus Muliebris"*.

1645. Caricature of a Fop. In a short doublet ...hes with ribbon loops and aglets. Long hair ...two love-locks. Patches on the face. *British Museum Single Sheet*.

153. 1645. Woodcut of a man in a short doublet, long Spanish hose. His boot-hose tops rest on the bucket-tops of the boots. *Broadside Single Sheet*.

154. 1640. Countrywoman with large hat, and high-heeled shoes with shoe-roses. *Hollar's Ornatus Muliebris"*.

155. *c.* 1650. Boy in a short loose doublet worn open, its slit sleeves showing an elegant shirt; small turned-down collar with band-strings. Shoulder belt for sword or rapier. Short breeches open at the knee and trimmed with ribbon loops known as "fancies" then very fashionable; thirty-six yards or more might be required. Boot-hose (unusual with shoes) slipping down. Ribbon shoe-strings.

156. 1649. The mother in a very low-necked dress with tight b[o] and long stomacher; wide stiff sleeves set in very low of[f] shoulders, then very fashionable. The child in a similar dress [with] leading strings, wearing an apron with bib and a coif. *De[l]* *Hopton and daughter by James Gandy, Royal Albert Me[m]* *Museum, Exeter.*

157 *left*. 1650–5. Woodcut of Shepherd in a loose doublet with short tabbed skirt and breeches trimmed with "fancies". His wife with veil head-dress and long dress. *Roxburghe Ballads.*

158 *right*. 1656. A Seller of Patches. "Here's black bags, Ribbons, Copper laces, Paintings and beauty spots for faces; Masques and Fans you here may have Taffity Gownes and Scarfs most brave, Curled haire and crisped Locks, Aprons white, and Holland Smocks; All sorts of powders here are sold To please all People young and old." *Roxburghe Ballads.*

1650–60. Little girl in a go-cart; she wears an apron [p]ointed bib pinned on; leading strings and lace-edged [ ] She holds a coral and bells (protection against witch-craft). *Norwich Castle Museum.*

160. 1663. "Musicks Hand-maide". A woodcut showing a lady playing; wearing a long-waisted gown very *décolleté* with a fashionable hair style; the gentleman in long doublet, breeches unconfined at the knee and canons (i.e. deep flounce to the top of the stocking). The attendant in simple dress and a deep gorget. *Victoria and Albert Museum.*

161. 1670–1700. Woodcut of a man and a woman. He is in a coat which is beginning to be waisted, with shoulder knot, cravat tied with cravat strings, and cocked hat. She is in a long-waisted open robe with a train and embroidered petticoat. *Contemporary woodcut.*

[ ]662. Charles II and his Queen. He wears petticoat [breech]es as introduced by him but rarely worn except at [court] from 1660's to 1670's. Trimming of "fancies". Short [jack]et and slashed sleeves. Stockings with deep flounces [or] "cannons", only worn with petticoat-breeches or [breech]es open at the knees. Shoes with stiff ribbon bows. [The] Queen in a gown, trained overskirt and puffed and [ ] sleeves sometimes called "virago sleeves". *Heath's Chronicle, British Museum.*

163. c. 1665–75. Woodcut. Family at table. Men in loose coats, square bib-like falling bands very fashionable in the 1660's; long hair and feathered hats worn indoors. The woman in a chaperone. The serving boy in doublet and full breeches. *Roxburghe Ballads.*

164. 1660–70. Catherine Gage in a day gown with circular *décolletage* and sleeves set in low off the shoulders. Fashionable hair style. *Christchurch Mansion, Ipswich.*

165. 1663. Lady in a large hat worn over a coif; round her n "whisk". "She shall have a rough demicaster with a sug crown, coifs. . . ."(1675. J. Dryden. "The Mistaken Husba The demicaster was a cheaper style of beaver hat. *Fount, Knoll, Somerset.*

166 *left*. 1670's. Gentleman in a loose coat with low pocket and sleeves and shoulder knot (a bunch of ribbons on the right shoulder). The latter was worn as an ornament from *c.* 1660 to 1700 and subsequently on liveries. His breeches are of the new style gathered in at the knees. *Hollar's "Hunting, Heroning and Fishing".*

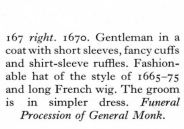

167 *right*. 1670. Gentleman in a coat with short sleeves, fancy cuffs and shirt-sleeve ruffles. Fashionable hat of the style of 1665–75 and long French wig. The groom is in simpler dress. *Funeral Procession of General Monk.*

168 *left* and 169 *right*. 1676. "Two Youths from the War with the Devil." The sober youth in puritanical clothes, the gay youth in fashionable dress including a tasselled handkerchief in his pocket, a feather in his hat and a cravat instead of the square falling band. He also has a long wig. *B. Keach's "War with ye Devil", Bodleian Library.*

170 *below right*. 1680–90. Woodcut of a man in a coat slightly waisted, with two vertical pockets, a feature borrowed from France; a cocked hat and curled wig. His shoes have the high square tongues in fashion from 1680 to 1720. *Roxburghe Ballads*.

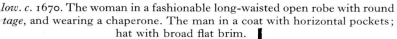

low. c. 1670. The woman in a fashionable long-waisted open robe with round *tage*, and wearing a chaperone. The man in a coat with horizontal pockets; hat with broad flat brim.

172 *top left*. 1695. James Stuar
Sister. The boy in a flared w
coat, fairly short sleeves with
cuffs; shoes with high sca
tongues, a style always turned o
show the red lining; a cravat
over stiffened cravat strings,
merely ornamental. He carr
feather-fringed three-cornered
His sister is in a trained gown
a lace apron front. Leading strin
hind. She wears a fontange head-
*Painting by Nicholas de Larg
National Portrait Gallery.*

173 *top right*. 1690. A boy aged
with a squirrel. He is dressed
girl; probably just before he
"breeched" which usually took
at the age of seven. *Master
Norwich Castle Museum.*

174 *left*. 1689. Satirical Print of C
I thrown overboard. A grou
common men in coats, cloak
Brandenburgs (large loose ove
which mainly replaced cloaks
1670). *Reproduced from
Museum Print.*

52

175. 1757–63. E. Rookes and family. The ladies in sacks, flounced petticoats and furbelow trimmings; wide *décolletage*. The man in a coat, waistcoat, three-cornered hat and physical wig. *A. Devis, Major and the Hon. Macdonald-Buchanan.*

PART FOUR

The Eighteenth Century

The art of the eighteenth century was imbued with a sense of order, and this now began to find expression in the design of dress. The elements of a costume composed a logical picture of relevant parts with subtle harmonies of colour. For the first time the skill of the tailor is apparent and elegance becomes the distinguishing feature of a gentleman's apparel.

True, it appears designed for static postures, not for activities; and Bentham in 1765, taking a long country tramp, complained that his satin breeches were "bitterly tight". Tight clothes, inviting unseemly disasters not uncommon among gentlemen of *ton* and tonnage, were thought "smart".

Fashions were constantly crossing the Channel both ways in spite of wars, England usually supplying new ideas and France new variations on them, but with this difference: the English gentleman freely adopted notions from his social inferiors, such as the Frock, the Flapped Hat, and the Buckskin Breeches; but these were not copied by the French gentleman until later.

During the first half of the century the components of a man's suit were often of the same material, cloth for day and silk or satin, laced and embroidered, for evening and ceremonial wear.

The collarless coat, close-fitting and waisted, had a flared skirt to the knees with three deep vents. The front was closed by buttons to the hem (until *c.* 1735) or to the waist (from 1720 on). Pockets had straight flaps to 1710 and later, scalloped. The sleeve had a variety of cuffs designed to indicate that the wearer was unaccustomed to doing manual work: large cuffs open behind, until 1750, or large and closed, the "Boot cuff" of the 1730's. Or the sleeves might be without cuffs, having a short side slit, buttoned.

The Frock, borrowed from the artisan from 1730 on, was a loose coat, never embroidered, with a flat turned-down collar, and no lapels; at first for informal wear and usually with metal buttons. The Waistcoat or Vest resembled the coat in cut, with skirts reaching nearly to the knees and sleeved, until the 1750's; sometimes it was double-breasted, and it was usually worn partly open to display the frilled shirt-front.

Knee-breeches were universally worn through the century, cut full in the seat and gathered into a waistband, the kneeband closed by a small buckle. The buttoned front closure persisted to 1750 but was then being replaced by front "falls".

With a frock the materials composing the three garments of the suit might all be different.

For négligée the Banyan or Indian Nightgown, resembling a loose knee-length coat wrapping over in front, was much worn.

For neckwear the Cravat (to 1740's) was a strip of linen or muslin loosely knotted under the chin, with falling ends, the Steinkirk being a cravat twisted on itself and threaded through a buttonhole of the coat. The Stock, from 1735, was a stiff folded neckband, and the Solitaire (1730's to 1770's) a length of black ribbon tied to the bag of the wig behind, the ends loosely fastened under the chin in front. The principal outdoor garment was the Surtout, a loose great-coat with a broad, capelike collar. Ample cloaks were also worn. Shoes had square blocked toes, high square heels, and high tongues, the toes becoming rounded and heels and tongues lower from 1740. Square or oblong metal buckles were small to 1730. Jackboots with bucket tops or half-jackboots ending below the knees were worn only on horseback. Stockings were "roll-ups" until 1750, a style discarded by young men by 1730.

The three-cornered hat (which Victorians called the "tricorne"), worn all through the century, was cocked in a variety of forms and often carried under the arm. The Round Hat, with brim not cocked, rigid or slouched, was less common. Wigs were worn by all classes, with or without a queue behind, the size diminishing by the middle of the century. "The grand distinguishing mark of a fine gentleman is the wearing of a sword" (*The Connoisseur*, 1754); but from 1730 it was being rivalled by the long malacca cane. After 1730 the frock replaced the coat for riding and sporting activities.

A woman's dress consisted of a gown and petticoat, the former comprising bodice and skirt in one, the latter opening in front to reveal the petticoat, and known as the Open Robe; less common was the closed robe. The separate jacket and skirt was a style much worn by the working woman.

A Bustle was worn to 1710, and revived from 1775, but much smaller. From 1710 to 1780 the conspicuous feature was the Hoop, of various shapes and sizes; the Bell Hoop, domed and small or large, 1710 to 1780; the Fan Hoop, 1740's and 1750's, pyramidal; and the Oblong Hoop, 1740's to 1760's, excessively wide but flat front and back.

In the Open Robe the bodice itself was usually open in front with the borders of the gap edged with bands of flat ruching ("Robings") and the opening filled in with stomacher. The closed bodice, rare except in the 1720' was buttoned down the front. Sleeves were about elbow length, ending in turned-up cuffs (1700 to 1750) o flounces (from 1740). The overskirt was trained to 1710 later, supported on a hoop.

Of open robes the Mantua (1700 to 1750) was a loos gown, the bodice unboned, the overskirt trained, an worn on all social occasions. The Nightgown was a ordinary open robe, the *décolletage* covered with som kind of neckwear, and worn for less ceremonial occasion Of Closed Robes, known later as Round Gowns, th Wrapping Gown (1735 to 1750) had a round *décolleta,* without robings and made with a wrapping front. C the bodice might be closed edge-to-edge down the from (1730's to 1740's), the top of the front of the skirt bein made with a short "fall".

The Sack (1720 to 1780) was capacious, falling from neck to hem like a bell tent until 1730; behind, small bo pleats stitched down to the neckband spread out in larg folds to the ground. The front was laced across the bosor The "Sack Back" (miscalled the "Watteau Pleat") con prised two double box-pleats on each side of the midlir back seam, and stitched down flat from neck to should level.

Of the separate bodice and skirt style there were sever varieties: (1) the bodice as a jacket (Fr. *Casaquin*) wi round basques; (2) the bodice as a short sack, the "Pete lair". The Riding Habit, of cloth, comprised jacket, wais coat resembling a man's, and petticoat. Outdoor garmen were mainly cloaks.

Indoor caps: the high fontange was succeeded by circular flat cap, the Pinner, and the Round-eared Ca (1730's to 1760's) which curved round the face to t level of the ears, with or without lappets. For undre wear the Mob Cap, with a puffed-out crown, was genera Out of doors, hoods, short or long, and small hats wit shallow crowns and narrow brims or with wide floppir brims, and also large flat straw hats with flat crown were worn through the first half of the century.

Hair ceased to be raised high after 1710 and curls at th sides and back of the head or curled all over behind, assiste by false curls, made the fashionable "Tête de Mouton"

Shoes had massive heels and pointed toes, the tongu high and square (to 1750).

In the second half of the century the modes of bot sexes appear to have been more youthful than those of th first. Men and, later, women, were becoming more addicte to outdoor activities. They were freely borrowing dres notions from their social inferiors who, in turn, wer eagerly imitating the modes of their betters, a safety-valv to the growing tension of class discontent. Our sublim gift of snobbery saved us, unlike the French, from a mor violent explosion.

Male costume developed a closer fit, with increasin display of the legs, the front skirts of the coat or froc being cut sloping back to end in front above the kne without a flare. A narrow standing collar was added to th coat from 1765, the sleeves close fitting with round cuf becoming small from 1770. The frock with its turned-down collar continued to be worn for informal occasions, but gradually, from 1770, was also worn ceremonially even at Court, when the collar rose to a high "stand-fall" from 1785. The frock was usually single-breasted to 1780, and then double-breasted with lapels.

The waistcoat, now sleeveless, became progressively shorter, the bottom horizontal, with or without a small stand collar and usually double-breasted. Under-waistcoats came into fashion in the 1790's. Breeches with small falls, and cut increasingly tight, reached well above the natural waist, supported by braces from 1790. The knee opening was closed by a buckle over the stocking, the buckles being often replaced by ties after 1780. Pantaloons or close-fitting tights ending at the ankles, appeared by 1790.

Coats were increasingly made of cloth, breeches of buckskin, and pantaloons of stockinette.

Of neckwear, the cravat was being replaced by the stock or neckcloth folded round the neck and stiffened with pasteboard. Wigs, with or without queues, were worn until the 1790's, tending to become smaller and, in the 1770's, often raised high above the forehead when the Exquisites known as the Maccaronis were influencing the fashions. It was a phase corresponding to the Aesthetic Movement of a hundred years later, and to it men owe the introduction of the inside breast-pocket in their coats.

The cocked hat continued in use, the Fantail form with back brim turned up, fashionable from 1780, and the Chapeau Bras carried under the arm (1770's on), but in addition the Round Hat, with round flat crown and wide brim, was becoming the mode for riding (from 1770's).

Female dress of the second half of the century comprised versions of the open robe, such as the Sack worn with its skirt open in front (1750 to 1780) and its bodice open or closed. The Trollopee (1750 to 1770) was a loose sack, the bodice without bones, the overskirt trained.

The English Gown, close-fitting to the waist, had a "Fourreau back" (the sewn-down back pleats converging to the waist but with the material continuing into the skirt). The Nightgown had now become a fashionable form for all occasions except when "full dress" was required. The Polonese, from 1770 to 1785, had an overskirt bunched up behind into three puffed draperies. From 1786 to 1794 the bodice of the open robe had a high waist, the front puffed out, and the skirt supported over a bustle.

The closed robe returned to fashion about 1780, sometimes in the form of a great-coat buttoned all down the front. In addition there was the separate bodice and skirt in the form of a jacket and waistcoat with a skirt.

From 1794 the Classical style, with high waist, no bustle, and usually of white materials with a minimum of underclothing, became the mode.

Of neckwear in the second half of the century the large square handkerchief draped over the *décolletage* in the 1780's, and puffed out like a pouter pigeon, was known as a Buffon. After hoops had been discarded (*c.* 1780's) outdoor garments comprised the three-quarter length Pelisse, the small hooded Polonese, and the green riding-coat or Joseph.

Indoor caps became bulkier, in the form of Mob caps, while "dress" caps were often quite small. Hats remained fairly simple until the 1770's, when the elaborate hair style caused them to become very large; in the 1780's the size was immense, such as the Devonshire hat immortalized by Gainsborough. The piled-up hair of the 1770's was an edifice adorned with flowers, vegetables and feathers, the back hair hanging in a flat loop or chignon.

Shoes with high Louis heels, pointed toes and buckles, remained the mode until the last decade when heels almost disappeared and buckles were replaced by ribbon rosettes. Short boots were worn out of doors, supported in muddy weather on pattens (a kind of wooden shoe standing on an iron ring).

176. 1785. In the Mall, St. James's Park. The ladies wear trained poloneses with flounced petticoats and the large hats then fashionable. *Coloured print by T. Day.*

177 *left. c.* 1710. A gentleman in a collarless coat with turned-up cuffs, shirt sleeves with lace ruffles, fancy waistcoat and the cravat loosely twisted and threaded through a buttonhole of the coat. Worn thus it was called a "Steinkirk". *Christchurch Mansions, Ipswich.*

178 *top right.* 1703. Lady in a long-waisted gown with stoma front and trained overskirt bunched up behind. On her he fontange cap fashionable from *c.* 1690 to 1710. *Woodcut from '* *Country Gentlewoman's Catechism".*

179. *c.* 1704. Woman riding pillion in a long-waisted gown with stomacher front and elbow sleeves with turned-up cuffs and head kerchief. The man in a "riding frock" or short coat with a flat turned-down collar, not fashionable until *c.* 1730; heavy jackboots and round hat. *Contemporary woodcut from Clarendon's "History of the Rebellion".*

180. *c.* 1710. William Leathes wearing a coat with fancy c matching waistcoat with scalloped pockets, a fashion just star A Steinkirk cravat; stockings rolled up over the breeches and h called "rollers" or "roll-ups". Shoes with square blocked *Lieutenant-Commander Robert Leathes, R.N.*

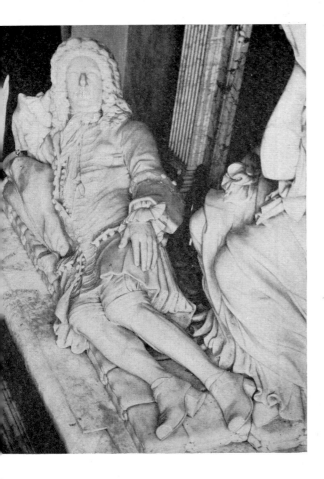

181 *top left*. 1720. Tomb of Sir R. Jennens. He wears coat and waistcoat with buttons to the hem. Roll-up stockings, shoes with high tongues and square-blocked toes, unfashionable after 1720, and a Steinkirk cravat. *Acton Church, Suffolk.*

182 *top right*. 1715. The Countess of Mar in a woman's riding habit consisting of a coat, waistcoat and "petticoat" (i.e. skirt), worn with a tricorne hat, wig, gloves and Steinkirk cravat. *Sir Godfrey Kneller. Earl of Mar and Kellie.*

183 *left*. 1710–20. A gentleman in a flared coat with long buttonholes, pocket flaps not scalloped (a fashion introduced *c.* 1710). His shoes have high tongues and small buckles. He carries a three-cornered ("tricorne") hat which could not be worn on a full-bottomed wig. *Loan Exhibition, Colchester, in 1951.*

184 *left*. 1715. Boy in a coat and sleeved waistcoat both cut
at the neck; belt for sword. Roll-up stockings. *Lord John 1
from the Orrery Papers.*

185 *right*. *c*. 1725. Sir Charles Blois in a coat with flared skirt and
three pleats from the "hip button"; scalloped pocket flap; shoes
with high tongues and rounded toes, a fashion then coming in.
Christchurch Mansion, Ipswich.

1718–20. 5th Viscount Irwin and Wife. She is in a jacket and petticoat over a dome-shaped hoop. (N.B. "petticoat" was the term ⎯ting the skirt, all through the eighteenth century.) He is in a coat with closed slit sleeves at the wrist and "long pockets" (i.e. vertical pockets); roll-up stockings and shoes with square blocked toes and high tongues. *Temple Newsam, Leeds.*

c. 1730. Card Party; the men in wigs except for the artist in a nightcap; the women in dresses with long tight bodices, elbow sleeves with plain cuffs and wearing small caps ("pinners"). *Gawen Hamilton, Walker Art Gallery, Liverpool.*

190 *top left*. 1735. Viscount Boyne in a coat with slit cuffs a
wrist, a style alternating with the boot-cuff in the 1730's.
breeches are buckled over the stockings, a fashion beginning t
place the "roll-ups". His wig with a small toupee (the toupee
a new mode). *After W. Hogarth, National Gallery of Scot*

191 *top right*. 1745–50. Gentleman at a writing-table. The
slit sleeves turned up to form cuffs, the waistcoat with trim
borders, and breeches buckled over the stockings, the garters b
visible. *A Devis, City of Birmingham Art Gallery.*

192 *left. c.* 1740. Francis Hayman, self portrait. He wears a "
yan" (a loose long coat as a négligé and later becoming a dress
gown), with a "nightcap" worn by day for comfort in place o
wig, over the clean-shaven head. His breeches have 4 or 5 bu
up the legs and he wears slippers. The term "mules" does
appear in the eighteenth century. *Royal Albert Memorial Mus
Exeter.*

1741. The Rev. Steynsham Master and his Wife; the latter in an open robe with a quilted petticoat, and on her head a "pinner", a small round cap. *A. Devis, Sir Brian Mountain.*

194 *left. c.* 1745. Husband and Wife. S tatting and wears a "petenlair" (short backed jacket) with fur borders and winged-cuffs; a neckerchief is caught i the top lacing over the stomacher. *E. School, Viscount Bearsted.*

195 *right.* 1742. 7th Viscount Irwin and Wife. The latter in a closed robe with pointed bodice and feather border to the *décolletage*. He is in an elegant coat, embroidered waistcoat, and breeches buckled over the stockings. *P. Mercier, Temple Newsam, Leeds.*

196. 1741. Colonel Charles Ingram, Son and Daughter, the two former wearing wigs. The son's coat has "mariner's cuffs" (with a vertical slit buttoned, and a turned-back cuff); his breeches are buckled over his stockings, whereas his father is wearing "roll-ups", now becoming old-fashioned. The daughter is in a back-fastening gown, apron with bib or "pinner", and a small round cap on the head. *P. Mercier, Temple Newsam, Leeds.*

197 *above left*. 1743. Mother (
Birch) and Daughter, the form
a front-fastening gown with
scalloped sleeves, lace ruffles
tucker. The child is simi
dressed. The mother's hair-sty
known as *tête de mouton* and the
ornament as a *pompon*, very fas
able throughout the 1740's and
the 1760's. *J. Highmore, Fitzw*
Museum, Cambridge.

198 *above. c.* 1745–50. Mother
Child, the former in a sack
gown with stomacher front
broad "robings", sleeves with
pleated cuffs, a fashion now b
ning; plain ruffles. Both mothe
child wear "round-eared c
"pinched" in the centre. *St*
Slaughter, National Gallery
Ireland.

199 *left. c.* 1745. Family Group
father and son in coats and e
waistcoats. The father wea
"physical wig". The mother
tight-bodied gown, neckerchie
round-eared cap. *Francis Ha*
Royal Albert Memorial Mu
Exeter.

66

right. 1745–50. Lady seated in a park. She s an open robe and quilted petticoat; elbow es with pleated cuffs; folded handkerchief the bosom. On the head a small round-cap. *A. Devis, City of Birmingham Art Gallery.*

201 *left. c.* 1740. Lady with a long neckerchief covering the stomacher and a long apron with matching lace. She wears a small round-eared cap. *Arthur Devis, City of Birmingham Art Gallery.*

202 *left*. 1740–5. Mrs. Elizabeth Ingram. Front-fastening g⌐
low *décolletage* with "modesty piece" and lace Medici collar, kn⌐
as a "medici". Dutch coiffure and pearl pompon. *Bartholo⌐
Dandridge, Temple Newsam, Leeds.*

203 *right*. 1743–5. Miss Fenton. An open robe with quilted petticoat worn over an oblong hoop; plain short robings and winged
cuffs which was a mode just starting. She has a transparent apron
and wears a round-eared cap and carries a bergère hat. *A. Devis,
C. Marshall Spink.*

1740–2. Mr. and Mrs. R. Bull. A family group, the women in stomacher-fronted gowns covered by neckerchiefs; the wife and daughter in aprons. The older women wear mobs tied under the chin. The little girl is in a round-eared cap. The father in a frock (i.e. a coat with a turned-down collar). The son is in a coat and light waistcoat. *A. Devis, Harris Art Gallery, Preston.*

205 *above. c.* 1745. A Family Group. The wom[en]
tight-bodied gowns and aprons; the older w[omen]
with mob caps and neckerchiefs, the young[er]
round-eared caps. The father and son standing be[hind]
him in coats and single-breasted waistcoats; th[e man]
on the right in a frock and double-breasted wais[tcoat]
and flapped pockets to his breeches. *Francis Hay[man.*
Leggatt Bros.

206 *left.* 1742. Daughters of Viscount Faucon[berg.]
Two little girls in low-necked gowns with back-fa[ll]-
ings. Short sleeves with up-and-down frills, a com[mon]
decoration on little girls' sleeves. *P. Mercier, Ca[t.]*
V. E. M. Wombwell.

207 *left. c.* 1747. Gentleman in murrey-brown velvet, the coat with wide falling cuffs, shirt sleeves with lace ruffles. A fringed waistcoat often worn as "dress" from 1720's to 1740's. He wears a wig with a toupee. *J. Highmore, Tate Gallery.*

right. 1740–50. Mary Pettus in a "wrapping-gown" over an ng hoop", the latter being wide from side to side. Lace ruffles to eeves. A "modesty piece" fills in the V of the *décolletage* which ged with a lace frill ("tucker"). Coiffure in the Dutch mode. *Norwich Castle Museum.*

210 *right*. 1745–50. The wife of the above. She is engaged in tatting and wears a round-eared cap, neckerchief and apron. *Francis Hayman, Tooth Galleries.*

1750's. Elinor Frances Dixie in a sack-back gown with treble sleeve-flounces now falling behind only and treble lace-edged ruffles. gauze handkerchief is confined by a "breast knot". She wears a bergère hat turned up front and back, a fashion of that decade, worn over an undercap. Note the long gloves. *H. Pickering, City of Nottingham Art Gallery.*

212. *c.* 1756. The Earl of Egmont and his Wife. The husband in a three-cornered hat and a physical wig; waistcoat worn open to di
the lace shirt-frill. His wife in a sack-backed gown and fashionable hat. "Every hat, whether of straw or silk, whether of the chamber
or mistress, must have the flaps turned up perpendicularly both before and behind." (1754. *The Connoisseur.*) *Sir Joshua Reynolds,
Agnew & Sons.*

213 *left. c.* 1750. A lady in a gown with embroidered robings and cuffs. (Rare for embroidered robings before 1750.) A plain stomacher, lace tucker and double lace ruffles to the chemise sleeves. Long gloves, Round-eared cap with lappets turned up. *W. Hogarth, Tooth Galleries.*

214 *right.* 1752. Mrs. Rowe, wife of Alderman Rowe. Wearing a fancy dress purporting to resemble a seventeenth century gown worn by an ancestor. The long sleeves were never a fashion of this date. Her hair style was known as the "Dutch Coiffure" as worn from 1730's to early 1750's. She has a small pompon. *H. Pickering, City of York Art Gallery.*

215 *left. c.* 1750. The Earl of Albemarle in a coat with wide spreading cuffs, satin waistcoat; wig with a toupee. *T. Hudson, Royal Albert Memorial Museum, Exeter.*

216 *right.* 1755–60. Mrs. Matthew Mitchell and children. The mother in a sack with wide stomacher and narrow robings; triple sleeve-flounces and ruffles; the petticoat trimmed with a flounce, a style now becoming fashionable, and "furbelows" (i.e. ruched ribbon which is also continued from the robings down to the hem). The girl in a plain gown; the boy in a sleeveless waistcoat, shirt and breeches. *T. Hudson, City of Leicester Art Gallery.*

1750's. Dr. Wathen and Family. The Doctor in a "physical wig" (a bushy bob wig worn by physicians). His wife in a gown with rative and very broad stomacher, the *décolletage* of the gown reaching to the tip of the shoulders, a style very fashionable at that date. gauze handkerchief" covers the bosom. The children are in gowns with leading strings and wear coifs. *George Knapton, City of Birmingham Art Gallery.*

218. *c.* 1760. The Duke of Grafton in a frock with the close long cuffs of that decade. *Attributed to Henry Walton, Walker Art Gallery, Liverpool.*

219. *c.* 1750. Lady on horseback wearing a masculine f█ (coat with collar) and waistcoat. The long skirt, then call█ "petticoat"; and feather-fringed three-cornered hat. ℱ█ *Wootton, Norwich Castle Museum.*

220. 1766. Group of young █ the first and third in coats █ low stand collars then cor█ into fashion; the second █ fourth in frocks, the last ha█ mariner's cuffs. All wear b█ solitaires (i.e. black ribbon v█ over the stock). *P. Ba█ Knoedler & Co.*

c. 1760. A youth, Jacob Morland, in a sporting coat with low stand collar and lapels, the latter seen only on sports coats or frocks at this date. The three-cornered hat given a sporting backward tilt. Socks are worn over the stockings. *G. Romney, Tate Gallery.*

222 *left.* 1761-2. Lord Willou
de Broke. Family Group.
husband in a frock and br
waistcoat and wearing a ty
with raised and forked toupe
the style of the 1760's. His wif
flounced and furbelowed
with ribbon neckband, Pu
cap and hair in rolled curls as
worn.   The· children in
décolleté dresses. *John Zo*
Lord Willoughby de Brof

223. 1767. Sir Robert Burdett wearing a suit of one material; a
black solitaire is worn over a white stock. The solitaire was usual
with a bag wig, a portion of which is visible. *Francis Cotes,*
Leggatt Bros.

224. 1762. Sir Robert Clayton. The coat with its low stand c
was then a new fashion. His wig with a slightly raised and fo
toupee was typical of the 1760's. *Thomas Gainsborough, Wc*
Art Gallery, Liverpool.

78

c. 1764. The grandmother in an open robe, quilted petticoat and dress apron, with hair-style of the period. The young woman in a small round cap, lace tippet and apron; the child wearing a small hat over a coif. *John Zoffany, Tooth Galleries.*

226 *left.* 1760's. Mrs. Cadoux in a trained sack gown, flounced and furbelowed. A small ruff at the neck. Hair raised on pads and a turban head-dress, then very fashionable. *Bristol School, Tate Gallery.*

227 *right. c.* 1763. Sir Francis Basset Bent, M.P. Wearing a frock with cuffs typical of the decade; a trimmed waistcoat; a wig with toupee slightly pointed over the forehead in the fashionable style of this decade. *Thomas Gainsborough, Bradford City Art Gallery.*

228 *below.* 1775–80. Shooting Party. Men in frocks, short waistcoats, tight breeches and round hats. One has striped stockings. Their natural hair is curled to resemble wigs. *John Zoffany, Tooth Galleries.*

229 *above*. 1776–8. The Beaumont Family. Men in frocks, waistcoats, breeches and tye-wigs. The lady with the raised coiffure of the period, a closed robe and draped skirt. *G. Romney, Tate Gallery.*

230 *left. c.* 1770. Thomas Nuthall in a sporting frock with four flapped pockets, waistcoat and breeches. His top boots are held up by "boot garters". His round hat now becoming fashionable for riding and sport. *N. Dance, Tate Gallery.*

231 *right*. 1770. Man wearing a frock and a double-breasted waistcoat of a cut worn for sport especially during the 1760's and early '70's. *Contemporary Print.*

232 *top*. 1777. John and Sophia Musters. Riding costumes, male and female. The man wears the fashionable round hat and club wig. *G. Stubbs, Col. J. N. Chaworth-Musters.*

233 *above*. 1787. A Milliner's Shop. "A seller of all sorts of private affairs to the ladies" in the shape of bustles, etc.

234. 1772. Colonel George Washington in the British [M]iform of the 22nd Regiment of Virginia. *Charles W[illiam] Peale, Washington and Lee University, Lexington, Vir[ginia.]*

235. *c.* 1780. "The Seven Dials," London. Country folk and artisans. The woman on the right, talking to a knife-grinder, wears a mob[,] a polonaise gown and "buffon" (i.e. a large neckerchief swathed round the shoulders and bunched out over the bosom). She also wea[rs an] apron. *Wm. Hodges, Tooth Galleries.*

Above. 1780's. Jonathan and Mary Walker of Ferham. The little girl in a frock with a broad sash. The boy in an adult style of suit with a double-breasted waistcoat. The open neck of the shirt is a childish feature. *Nottingham City Art Gallery*.

Right. c. 1780. "The Elopement". The country girl in a large hat over a cap and hooded cloak. The man in a military frock and tight breeches; cocked hat with cockade, and light jack-boots. The servant in a round hat and top-boots. *From a print by R. Smith after G. Morland*.

1789–90. The Anglers' Repast. The ladies in riding-coat dresses and hats. The men in frocks, round hats and top-boots (also known as "jockey boots"). *From Print of Mezzotint by Wm. Ward after G. Morland*.

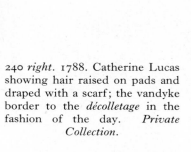

239 *left*. 1785–8. Lady in a wig with roll curls on the neck and wearing a small day cap; buffon neckerchief. *Private Collection*.

240 *right*. 1788. Catherine Lucas showing hair raised on pads and draped with a scarf; the vandyke border to the *décolletage* in the fashion of the day. *Private Collection*.

241. *c*. 1785. The Caddick Family Group. Men in frocks and tye-wigs. One has a double-breasted waistcoat, another a striped, stripes very fashionable in that decade. The lady is in a fashionable hat with its brim "which falls down like the roof of a house". *Arthur Cac Walker Art Gallery, Liverpool.*

242. 1786. Sir Christopher and Lady Sykes. He is in a frock with high turned-down collar, and breeches buckled below the knees with an oval buckle as customary in the 1780's for "undress". She is in a plain *décollete* open robe with long tight sleeves, a fashion introduced in the 1780's. *George Romney, Sir Richard Sykes.*

243 *left*. 1786. "Autumn". Coloured print of a lac
gown with overskirt and tight long sleeves whicl
superseded the elbow-sleeves hitherto worn throu
the century. The shoes have the fashionable Italian
Large hat. The man wears the fashionable double-b
waistcoat. *Contemporary Print*.

244 *right*. 1786. "Winter". Coloured print showing a
man in a military style frock, double-breasted waistcoat, and bicorne hat (i.e. cocked front and back)
fashionable from 1780's. He wears a fringed sash
("Burdash"). The lady is in a pelisse and wears a large
cocked "riding hat". The child is in a great coat.
Contemporary Print.

1786. Mrs. Wilbraham Bootle wearing a fur-edged "pelisse" (in the eighteenth century this was a voluminous cloak with arm-and a deep falling collar or hood). Her hair is raised on pads and she wears a small draped cap, muff and long gloves. *Portrait by Romney, National Gallery of Scotland.*

246 *above. c.* 1790. The Pai
Household. The lady in an
robe, and wearing an a
a small "poking bonnet"
mittens. The men are in fr
one being in military uni
J. Zoffany, Mrs. Mario
Hughes.

247 *left.* 1796. "Two-p
Whist." Caricature. The w
in mob caps and one in a
The men have the short st
queues as worn in the 1
Caricature by J. Gilray

ght. 1790. "A Jessamy". Caricature of a Fop in a short frock—then beginning to be called a *-coat*"—a short horizontally striped waistcoat and stockings. The long breeches are tied with ribbon rosettes. Large fob ribbons. Bicorne hat. Club wig. *From "The Follies of Man".*

elow. 1795–1800. The Sayer Family Group. The ladies in high-waisted long gowns and small round bonnets; shoes without heels. The men in frocks and tight breeches. *J. Zoffany.*

250. *c.* 1793. Viscountess Cren
in a trained gown with long
sleeves and large mob cap. Not
after 1794 the waist became
Sir Thomas Lawrence, Lt.-
mander C. Windham.

251. 1815–20. The Hicks Children. The two younger boys in "skeleton suits"; the older in a tail coat and trousers. All wear small ruffs. The girl in a very high-waisted dress. *Margaret Carpenter, Leger Gallery.*

PART FIVE

The Nineteenth Century

With an abundance of materials increasing in variety and quality the range of the fashionable world now came to include all who were comfortably off in the middle class. "Fashion" was becoming, in fact, the taste of the prosperous, especially from the middle of the century on.

Progress towards more rational forms was far more marked in male than in female costume; men seeking to advance in that direction might seem to lack gentlemanly refinement, but women attempting to do so, especially those daring to borrow male garments, were condemned as immoral. On the other hand the niceties of dress were perhaps more closely studied than hitherto, with changes of clothing four or five times a day, under strict conventions as to what might or might not be worn on particular occasions.

There were few signs of rational progress by either sex before the Crimean War, which conferred on men an inestimable blessing: the belief that one might be comfortably clad and yet look like a gentleman. The second half of the century was occupied in developing this novel idea, while audacious young women followed in man's footsteps and often in his clothes.

As the century opened the Napoleonic war was raging and male fashions, imitating the military, displayed the high-collared cutaway coat and high-waisted breeches, often replaced by pantaloons to the ankles. For informal wear trousers appeared in 1807. With high stock above a frilled shirt-front head movement was restrained. But manners declined; it became "quite the tippy" to look slovenly and to imitate the manners of coachmen. "The present race of Bucks without blood, Beaux without taste, and Gentlemen without manners" (*The Morning Chronicle*, 1800) was a wartime product. The cutaway coat, known as a "dress coat", was worn buttoned up for formal occasions by day, and left open for evening wear; terms used until the mid-century. The "frock coat" was a name now applied only to a full-skirted collared coat without cut-in or slope, and originally a military garment.

Trousers, pleated into a waistband and immensely wide in the leg, known as "Cossacks", appeared in 1814. Fashionable footwear was the Hessian boot, calf-length, and indoor shoes with pointed toes and low heels. Top-boots were worn with breeches and Half-boots (to just above the ankles) with pantaloons. The Round Hat with a tall and straight-sided crown was in general use, the forerunner of the Victorian "top hat". Wigs were no longer the mode, the hair being dishevelled *à la militaire*.

The reign of the Dandies (1820 to 1850), led by Count D'Orsay, marked by excessively tight clothing over tight corsets as the distinguishing feature of the gentleman, saw in 1823 a seam at the waist introduced into the skirted coat, and in 1843 the "side bodies" at the back, both devices to enhance the closeness of fit. The legs of pantaloons, fitting like a glove, required straps under the insteps.

By 1825 the riding coat, known later as a "Newmarket", resembling a short frock coat with the fronts sloping away, began to appear, the prototype of the (modern) morning coat, and in fact often worn as such.

Throughout the second quarter of the century, although the design of male costume was becoming more architectural in spirit, the pictorial influence remained strong; a day costume might be polychromatic in its mixture of colours to which multiple waistcoats and linings of cloaks added variety; a bright blue coat, purple waistcoat and canary trousers would blend cheerfully at breakfast, and in evening dress gentlemen would glow with coloured stones and Venetian chains. Male legs were still fascinating objects though ladies shrank from naming the garment containing them, employing such euphemisms as "unmentionables" or "inexpressibles".

It is noteworthy that it became a rule for the lower half of the male costume to be lighter in colour than the top half, in order to "catch the eye", whereas in female dress the opposite was the rule. Thus the spectator's eye was drawn to male legs but to the female "figure".

The chimney-pot silk hat had banished the beaver in the 1840's and as a symbol of gentility towered higher and higher. The hair was worn long and curled with short whiskers. For outdoor wear cloaks were fashionable, while in 1836 there appeared a portent of democracy— "a sort of smockfrock of Mackintosh's Indiarubber cloth. . . . No one can look like a gentleman in such a garb and it is of a most unpleasant odour."

A modish garment was the Chesterfield overcoat, waisted and without a seam at the waist.

Female dress during the first twenty years of the century retained traces of its Classical form now petrified into a high waist and rigidly narrow skirt often of cotton, the breasts thrust upwards by tight stays. The dress was a frock with bodice and skirt in one, for day, or with an over-tunic for evening, the train of the latter disappearing after 1812. Small bustles began to return to fashion at this time and Gothic trimmings soon overlaid the Classical form.

More significant was the fact that those muslin and cotton dresses were very cheap, and for the first time in our history it became possible for all classes to indulge in the latest fashions. Mistress and maid dressed alike, and, with "nudity" the mode, it was hard to distinguish milliners from duchesses. Actually it was not "nudity" so much as "transparency" over a minimum of under-clothing that was practised.

After the war years a romantic revival of Tudor modes together with extreme tight-lacing, produced an hour glass outline exaggerated by ballooned sleeves an widening skirts. As a result young women of the 1830' have an exuberant air and look as though they woul *bounce* well. Very different was the appearance of th 1840's, weighed down by ladylike languor and a load o petticoats. A tight-fitting bodice and sleeves and the grip of long tight stays checked any unseemly activities indeed the armholes were so small and the sleeves set i so that the arm could not be raised above the head, a clea proof of their genteel incapacity. Charmingly statuesque i the 1840's, who would have supposed that ten years late Galatea, come to life, would be earning the opprobriou title of "fast"?

Certainly 1848—"the Year of Revolution"—wit thrones toppling all over Europe, had a disturbing effect reflected in the fashions of the day. A new vitality appeare in gentlemen's clothes, with notions borrowed from th lower classes; in particular, a looser, more comfortabl garment than the skirted coat, in the form of a long kin of jacket—"a baggy sac" known as a Tweedside, th forerunner of the modern Lounge jacket.

Likewise, for country wear the gentleman began to us a cloth cap such as only the artisan and schoolboy ha worn since Tudor days. The Crimean war emphasized to those serving, the disadvantages of tight clothing, an henceforth men's fashions illustrate a struggle betwee the traditional "smartness" of tight-fitting garment impeding mobility but indicative of superior social class and the comfort and flexibility of a looser fit, such a favoured by the worker. The principal exponents wer the frock coat and morning coat, on the one hand, an the lounge suit on the other. In spite of all resistance th latter eventually won, though a World War was neede for the victory. Even today in the garb of the Ancien Order of Gentlemen may be seen bridegrooms, painfull smart. . . .

The 1850's saw the gradual extinction of the da "dress coat", and trousers expanding into "peg-tops" earned the name of a "pair of bags". The male leg once so captivating, now in the dim eclipse of a disastrou twilight ceased to count; indeed the hero of the popula novel henceforth was allowed no physical attractio beyond being "clean-limbed".

It was being said (*Tailor & Cutter*, 1878) that "dres in our day has ceased to be the index of a man's socia position". This was largely due to his activities in th field of sport, where such garments as knickerbockers an Norfolk jacket (from the 1870's on) marked an advanc in comfort and utility at the cost of discarding symbols o class distinction. And while the lounge suit increased i popularity the formal garments, frock coat and mornin coat, were themselves rivals, sometimes one and some times the other being thought the smarter. In spite o the efforts of the Best People and the strained elegance o the Masher the lament was echoed on all sides: "We ar threatened with a general decadence in dress" (1894) "So great is the modern tendency to sacrifice appearanc comfort that before long it is feared the silk hat will ly be seen in the City and Piccadilly" (1899). Already e gentleman's dress suit had become a deadly monotony ich he shared with the waiters; would the same fate ertake the great invention of the nineteenth century, e lounge suit?

During the first half of that century Woman's costume emed to assume that for the most part she was an door creature, but from 1850 she began to emerge erpoweringly in skirts steadily expanding until in 1856 ey needed the support of a wire cage, the artificial rinoline". Here was a device which suited the erect ving figure rather than the seated. Its function, we d, was "to keep the common herd at arm's length, or her, at petticoat's breadth", but presently it was short ough to reveal ankles and more.

Young women—or parts of them—were emerging from ir cage, and evening dresses were alarmingly *décolleté*. 1863 the English "walking dress", designed expressly permit active outdoor exercise, was an innovation never herto dreamed of. At the same time the bonnet, with its e-blinkers limiting vision to the narrow path ahead, s being replaced by the hat allowing vision to roam. The 1870's saw the trained day dress replace the noline, but in 1878 a sign of the times was the "tailor-de costume", designed on masculine lines. That it s apparently devoid of any suggestion of sex appeal s indeed a new conception of female dress. This glish banner of emancipation appealed only to a nority. Most women shrank from the horrid prospect, ferring to display themselves as charmingly ineffective atures swathed in trained hobble-skirts or exploiting

the components of a "good figure, namely a well-developed bust, tapering waist, and large hips".

Emancipation called for protection, and in the 1880's women were heavily guarded by clothing, up to a couple of stones' weight in winter, the indoor dresses apparently wrapped in antimacassars and trimmed with dead animals including insects and reptiles, while every species of bird decorated the headgear.

While the lady of fashion was covering herself with zoological charms, emancipated young women in tweed tailormades indulged in walking tours, tennis, and tricycling. In the hunting field the side-saddle was still *de rigueur*.

The desire to disguise the natural shape of the body, which seems inherent in the feminine mind, took the form in the 1880's of wearing enormous bustles. Equally disguising, in a sense, was the prevailing colour taste which would allow a mixture of three or four unrelated colours to compose a dress. "Never was more art displayed in the amalgamation of colours. . . ."

The gored skirt of the 'Nineties was one of the most original dress-designs of the century, overshadowed though it was by the gigantic sleeves of the jacket and blouse (1895-6). This skirt in its many forms ingeniously constructed, led at the close to the yoked skirt, and thence to the flared.

A progressive feature was the bicycling costume, whether as "divided skirt" or as "bloomers", for now at last Woman had become a recognizable biped. The fashionable dress designer was beginning to perceive with a sigh, that many women were now demanding more rational clothes. The question for the twentieth century to solve was—how was Woman to look rational and yet be charming?

252. 1828. The women wear low-necked day dresses. The man wears a Wellington top-hat. Scene from the comedy of "Paul Pry". *Painted by George Clint.*

253 *above*. 1800. London full dresses trained and worn with feath
bonnets and large muff. *A fashion plate.*

254 *top left*. 1804. Man in overcoat, short striped trousers not yet
by gentlemen but from mid-eighteenth century on by artisans, sa
etc., and boys. Note his large hat. *Townsend the Bow Street Runn
R. Dighton.*

255 *left*. 1804. Robert Southey's coat-collar has the "M cut" bet
it and the lapel, a style of cut not seen before 1803. He wears
pantaloons with ankle slits. *Drawing by H. Edridge, 1804, Na
Portrait Gallery.*

right. 1807. Fashion Plate of morn-
[wal]king costumes. The lady in a
[pelis]se and hat worn over a cap. The
[gent]leman in closed double-breasted
[coat], pantaloons, Hessian boots, and
top hat. *Le Beau Monde.*

top right. 1808. Fashion Plate of
["full dress"]. The gentleman in
[trou]sers, tail-coat worn open, and waist-
[coat] with stand-step collar and very high
[nec]k. The lady in a high-waisted dress
[with] vandyked borders, long gloves and
[a] scarf cloak. *Le Beau Monde.*

below. 1807. Fashion Plate. The
[gent]leman in evening dress, a blue tail-
[coat] with gilt buttons and breeches;
[unde]r his arm a folded crescentic
["cha]peau bras". The lady next to him is
[in e]vening dress; the second lady in
[eve]ning dress with cloak and turban.
Le Beau Monde.

below right. 1808. Fashion Plate.
[Two] walking dresses and one opera
[dres]s. The lady on the left in a fur-
[trim]med pelisse and cap, arm in arm
[with] a gentleman in a greatcoat fastened
[with] brandenburgs and wearing Hessian
[boot]s. The lady on the other side in
[an] opera dress. *Le Beau Monde.*

260 *above*. 1816. Lord Grantham in morning dress, a double-breasted tail-coat with "M" collar and very long sleeves; pantaloons and Hessians; top hat; very high collar; cravat popularly known as a "starcher". *Drawing by J. A. Dominique Ingres, Major Edward Compton.*

261 *top right*. *c.* 1812–14. Diana Countess of Normanton in a high-waisted dress with short puffed sleeves as worn by day. *Sir Thomas Lawrence, Earl of Normanton.*

262 *right*. 1800–5. Boy in a "skeleton suit"; the trousers buttoned to the coat and the front with "whole falls" and ankle-slits. The deep frilled turned-down collar was worn by small boys. *John Opie, Leicester City Art Gallery.*

63. *c.* 1810. Sir David Wilkie. Wearing a flowered banyan over pantaloons which are unbuttoned at the ankles; his feet in mules.
Andrew Geddes, Scottish National Portrait Gallery.

264 *above left.* 1818. Lord Lake in a greatcoat and pantaloon-trousers. *Drawing by R. Dighton.*

265 *above right.* 1812. Fashion plate of Riding costume. A green riding habit ornamented "*à la militaire*". Small black beaver riding hat with green ostrich feather, black half-boots laced and fringed with green. York tan gloves.
La Belle Assemblée.

266 *left.* 1819. Colonel Jollyffe in an "undress" tail-coat, waistcoat with step-stand collar; a "starcher" round the neck; breeches and gaiters; a round hat turned up at the sides. *Drawing by R. Dighton.*

267 *right.* 1813. Fashion plate of a Lady's walking dress. A stone-coloured habit trimmed with swansdown. "The waist much shorter than they have been worn for some time." Fur "Regency hat", black kid sandals. "Some elegantes wear silk stockings to correspond with the habit; but white are more general."
La Belle Assemblée.

above. 1819. Caricature of "Dandies in Rotten Row". The men wear Petersham "Cossacks" (baggy-legged trousers) and Jean de Bry ts with short tails and puffed-up shoulders; the very high "pillory collars" with corners known as "winkers" are surrounded by starched cravats. *Victoria and Albert Museum.*

ight. 1814. Bathing at Bridling-ay, Yorks. The women in long l bathing-gowns being dipped sea by the bathing-women. *ustration by George Walker*

270 *above. c.* 1820. The Palmer Family. The husband in a countrified sporting coat, breeches and gaiters. His wife in a high-waisted gown with wadded hem, a mode of the 1820's. She wears a mob cap. *James Leakey, Royal Albert Memorial Museum, Exeter.*

271 *left.* 1819. Charles Matthews in a box coat (i.e. overcoat with cape) and a striped waistcoat with step-stand collar. His high shirt-collar was often called a "pillory collar". *Contemporary illustration.*

ight. 1818. Going to church. The lady in a high-waisted —e, large bonnet and scarf; the gentleman in the early form —e nineteenth-century frock coat. *Illustration in "Princess Charlotte" by R. Huish. Published* 1818.

below. "Monstrosities of 1816. Scene in Hyde Park." —men wear three styles of Cossack trousers and the figure —e extreme right has an early form of frock coat. The —n show extreme *décolletage* with short waists, short skirts —vo have the stooping stance known as the "Grecian bend". *Caricature by George Cruikshank.*

274 *left*. 1821. Fashion plate of a "promenade dress", a dark violet pelisse trimmed with satin bells; a cashmere shawl, lace ruff and shady bonnet. Boots of violet kid. Limerick gloves, ermine muff. *Ackermann's Repository*, 1821.

275 *right*. 1821. A City gentleman in an undress tail-coat, breeches and a hat in the shape known later as a "bowler". *Drawing by R. Dighton*.

276 *left*. 1823. Mr. Lowe in undress tail-coat, breeches, top-boots buttoned to the breeches, and top-hat. *Drawing by R. Dighton*.

277 *right*. 1824. Fashion plate of walking dress, a pelisse of rose-coloured silk, the collar surmounted by a ruff of Erling's lace. She carries a reticule and wears a black velvet hat. "*The World of Fashion*".

278 *left*. 1824. Fashion plate of a blue satin evening dress and violet fur-lined evening cloak called a "Swedish mantle". On the head a toque trimmed with feathers. White satin shoes. "*The World of Fashion*".

279 *right*. 1824. Fashion plate of a yellow ball-dress, the waist now in the natural position; the skirt with puffing round the hem; the evening turban is trimmed with feathers. Long gloves. "*The World of Fashion*".

280 *left*. 1825. Fashion plate of a dinner dress of "gros de Naples, the colour of pomegranate rind". Hair with Apollo knots decorated with a diadem and "glauvina pins". White satin shoes; white kid gloves. *Ibid*.

281 *right*. 1825–6. Fashion plate of Mother and Daughter in party dresses; the mother's with padded hem. The little girl wears pantalettes.

282 *left*. 1827. Fashion plate of a wedding dress. The dress resembles an evening dress with moderate *décolletage* but with sleeves to the wrists. The hair is dressed with Apollo knots and the bridal veil hangs down behind. (This was not worn over the face until the 1860's. "*The World of Fashion*".

283 *right*. 1825. Fashion plate of a gentleman in a blue dress-coat with gilt buttons and velvet collar; vest and under-vest; and flesh-coloured breeches. An opera hat or chapeau bras under the arm. 1825. Fashion Plate of a man's double-breasted greatcoat worn over a double-breasted morning tail-coat and trousers. *Cyclopaedia of British Costume by Hearne, reproduced in B. Gile's (1825) "History of the Art of Cutting in England*".

284 *below*. 1822. Caricature of a Country Wedding. The bridegroom in a tail-coat, breeches, and top-boots. Note the spurs which were fashionable "on every kind of boot, even by those who never sit on a horse in their lives". (1829. "*Gentleman's Magazine of Fashion*.") His bride is in a white dress, pelisse and bonnet. *Caricature by W. Heath*.

285 *left*. 1824. Mr. Lindsey in undress tail-coat, strapped trousers, very high shirt collar and black stock. *Drawing by R. Dighton.*

286 *right*. 1824. The butcher boy in breeches with whole falls, apron, stockings, and short boots known as "highlows". The gentleman in the early form of short frock coat with high rolled collar and "M" cut. Strapped trousers. *Caricature by R. Dighton.*

287 *below left*. 1828. A Housemaid. Her dress is of a fashionable design with gigot sleeves. She wears a mob cap and an apron. The costume is very similar to that worn by Mary, the charming housemaid in *The Pickwick Papers* as depicted by "Phiz" in 1837. *Drawing by W. Heath.*

288 *below right*. c. 1829. A domestic cleaning a stone floor with mop and bucket. For this she wears on her feet iron-ringed pattens which keep her feet out of the wet. The short skirt is evidently supported behind on a bustle which at this date had become very large. Pattens continued to be used in this way to the end of the century. *Drawing by W. Heath.*

289 *left. c.* 1828. Caricature ridiculing the feminine fashions of that day.
pinched-in waist by excessive tight-lacing, the gigot sleeves and short skirt
especially the gigantic hat were features much attacked in caricatures,
"Not content with excessive tight lacing our ladies of fashion pad themse
till they resemble bottle-spiders." The hats trimmed with some sixty yard
of polychromatic ribbons cause: "horses to shy and dogs to bark", and the b
ram linings of the huge sleeves produced such a rustling noise that in a draw
room of ladies, speech was inaudible above the din. *Drawing by W. He*

290 *below. c.* 1829. Caricature depicting the extremes of tight-lacing as effe
by an imaginary machine. The fashion was widespread; a tradesman in
complained that his daughters "are unable to stand, sit or walk as women
to do. To expect one of them to stoop would be absurd. My daughter Mar
made the experiment the other day; her stays gave way with a tremen
explosion and down she fell . . . and I thought she had snapped in two". *Dra*
by W. Heath.

291 *left*. 1829. Fashion plate of a walking dress and a carriage dress. The former has a *canezou-fichu* over the shoulders while the latter has a *canezou-pélerine*, the ends tucked under the belt; and above the top of the chemisette is a ruff. With a carriage dress the hat is adorned with a veil which hangs down behind and at the sides. *La Belle Assemblée*.

...ight. 1827. A promenade dress, a pelisse with gigot sleeves, ...ith a large hat draped with lace. *Ackermann's Repository*.

293 *above*. 1826–9. Children of
Walter, Esq., of Bear Wood. The elde
in an Eton jacket, trousers with split
the younger boys in tunics and trot
The little girl in a frock with gigot sle
large "village hat" over a day cap, a
wearing sandal shoes. *Portrait at*
Wood. See No. 298.

294 *left*. 1830. "Mermaids at Brighto
bathing gowns of flannel with caps, as
used for seaside bathing. *Drawing b*
Heath.

above. 1830–6. Lady Blessington in a day dress with
"onna Maria" sleeves and a "Babet" cap. *Drawing by
D. Maclise.*

above centre. c. 1830. A clergyman in a short flared
ble-breasted frock coat, trousers without straps, and
top hat. From this date on the frock coat was one of
principal body-coats of the century. *Drawing by
D. Maclise.*

above right. 1830–6. Anna Maria Hall in a day dress
large "imbecile" sleeves, sash belt, buckled, and
ing across her forehead the fashionable ornament
known as a *ferronière*. *Drawing by D. Maclise.*

ight. 1834–5. John Walter II in a frock coat, close-
g trousers, and a velvet waistcoat. *Portrait at Bear
Wood. See 293.*

299 *left.* 1833. An evening dress with low-cut bodice and beret sleeves; full skirt rather short; hair dressed with an Apollo knot. *Fashion Plate, Victoria and Albert Museum.*

300 *right.* 1838–9. Thomas Raikes in a frock coat and "railroad trousers", the latter fashionable from 1837 to 1850, the stripes often vertical only but sometimes horizontal as well. *Frontispiece to "Raike's Journal", ed.* 1856.

301 *below. c.* 1830. "Old Cheltenham Characters." Gentlemen in various contemporary styles of dress; in day "dress-coats", frock c and overcoats. No. 4 wears a Petersham or caped overcoat. No. 18 wears a Pilot or Pea Jacket, a recent fashion, double-breasted and with several pockets; worn for sport or for riding (this gentleman wears spurs) and could be used as an overcoat or as a body-coat. *by R. Dighton, Cheltenham Museum.*

ight. 1843. Showing men's evening dress styles; the first
 in a tail-coat, white waistcoat with roll collar and panta-
; the second in tail-coat, figured waistcoat and breeches.
 wear gloves. These suits are of black cloth; the blue
ng dress-suit with gilt buttons was going out of fashion.
Practical Guide for the Tailor's Cutting-Room", by J. Couts.

ottom right. 1843. Men in morning suits, double-breasted
ats worn closed; strapped trousers. *"A Practical Guide*
for the Tailor's Cutting-Room", by J. Couts.

elow. 1840. Lady Chesterfield in a low evening dress, the
with long side ringlets, the back hair tied back and falling
 in ringlets as well. *Drawing by Count D'Orsay.*

305 *top left*. 1843. The sportsman in a shooting j
breeches and gaiters, and carrying a gun; the friend, s
is in a "morning gown". "*A Practical Guide for the T*
Cutting-Room", *by J. Couts.*

306 *top right*. 1843. The coachman in a box coat with mu
capes; the other figure is a jockey in riding kit. *loc. c*

307 *left*. 1843. A Page and a Tiger. The latter, now ex
was a boy who sat precariously at the back of a fashic
phaeton or similar vehicle and served to hold the h
heads etc.; a kind of "outdoor page-boy" in fact. *loc.*

308 *below*. 1843. Gentleman in dress riding clothes, a
coat, double-breasted waistcoat, scarf neckcloth, str
trousers and top hat. *Drawing by Count D'Orsay*

309 *left*. 1843. Miss Craven wearing an evening dress with pointed bodice, low *décolletage* and lace "bertha"; full skirt. The evening gloves are wrist-length only and are trimmed with ribbon ruching. She has a large evening handkerchief. The hair with long side ringlets. *Steel Engraving.*

310 *right*. 1843. Two boys, the younger on the left in an Eton suit and peaked cap; the older boy in a frock coat and holding a top hat. Both wear strapped trousers and gloves. "*A Practical Guide for the Tailor's Cutting-Room*", by *J. Couts.*

311 *below*. 1843. Three boys; the one with a hoop wears a skeleton suit. The other two are in tunics and trousers. One wears a "quartered cap". "*A Practical Guide for the Tailor's Cutting-Room*", by *J. Couts.*

312 *above*. 1842. Gentleman in a frock coat, the long sleeves with slit cuffs; a flowered waistcoat, scarf-tie and tie-pin. *W. Huggins, Walker Art Gallery, Liverpool.*

313 *left*. 1845. An Alderman in a frock coat, double-breasted waistcoat with wide lapels, and close-fitting trousers; the boots with square toes. He wears the substantial neckcloth of the period. *Manchester City Art Gallery.*

right. 1852. Fashion plate. The
with a parasol is in a dress with
uine bodice and pagoda sleeves,
skirt with multiple flounces.
lady on the right wears a
co bodice and waistcoat front.
'The World of Fashion''.

top right. c. 1853. Mrs. Howard
in a riding habit over a white
petticoat. *Song Cover.*

below. 1847. "The Eleven of
nd" in cricket costumes. *From a
ured lithograph publ. in* 1847.

317 *left*. 1859. In an excu
train, the men and women v
ing shawls; the women in bo
worn far back; the older m
top hats, and a young man
soft broad hat of the
popularly known as a "brim
*C. Rossiter, City of Birmin
Art Gallery.*

318 *below*. 1858. Archery group. The men in a wide variety of sports wear. The little girl in the centre has a crinoline to support the
and wears a pork-pie hat. The ladies wear the "round hats" very fashionable in that decade. The old gentleman in an old-fashioned b
brimmed hat, a contrast to that worn by the youth in a tall hat of the style then fashionable. *Original photograph.*

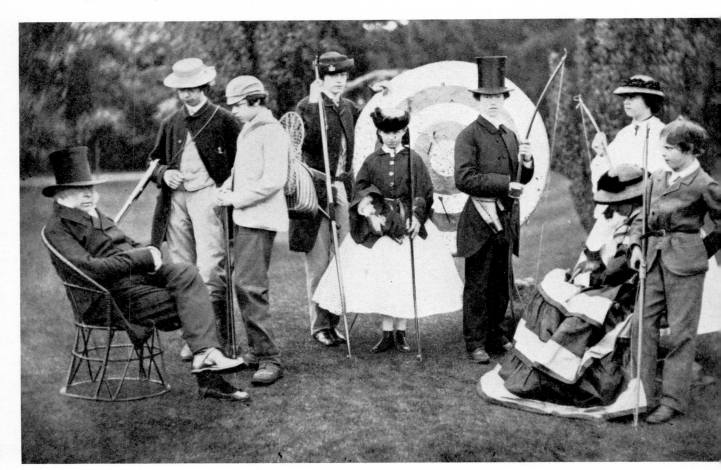

right. 1857. "Eastward Ho!" The
...en in shawls and bonnets worn far
... on the head exposing the centre-
...ng of the hair, a fashion adopted by
...etween 1853 and 1858. *H. N. O'Neil,
Sir Richard Proby.*

...bottom right. 1858–60. The seated
...eman is in a light-coloured top hat,
... wears elastic-sided boots. The centre
... is in a braided frock coat with wide
...s. The third man wears a morning
... commonly known at that date as
...hooting coat"—from which it was
...ed. This "shooting coat" was worn
...hers than sportsmen, for example by
...eli when he made his celebrated
...ss at Oxford in 1864. The name
...ned in use until *c.* 1890. *Original
photograph.*

...eft. c. 1856–7. Lady in a summer
... with high bodice, bell sleeves and
...antes (under-sleeves) and a skirt
... multiple flounces worn over a
crinoline. *From a photograph.*

117

322 *above*. 1860. John Baldwin Buckstone we
a frock coat and double-breasted waistcoat
wide lapels buttoned back, and large sprea
bow-tie. *Steel engraving.*

323 *left*. 1858. John Ellis, Chairman of the
land Railway Co., in the dress of the day, we
an overcoat. *Steel engraving.*

right. 1861. Princess Alice in a crinoline dress with pagoda ...es and *engageantes* (white under-sleeves). The rosettes ... the front were a fashion of this year. *Engraving by D. J. Pound.*

...ottom right. 1862. A large crinoline dress and lace shawl. The ...with two loose ringlets as worn by young women. *Engraving by W. Alais.*

...elow. 1860. Full length portrait of the Earl of Abergavenny ...frock coat, the dark coat and waistcoat contrasting with the ...r trousers. This was the rule for men's costume, whereas ...women's it was the reverse with the upper half of the costume ...as a blouse) always lighter than the skirt. *From a photograph.*

327 *above*. 1865–8. "The Free Seat." The old m
rustic breeches and laced shoes. The young m
trousers and boots having "eyelet hooks" for
up, a quite recent fashion. The young woman
a hat and a large shawl. The old woman and
are in sun-bonnets and the mother has a small far
bonnet. *Y. Lobley, City of Birmingham Art G*

328 *left*. 1861. "Looking for the Mail Packet." I
"Conversation Picture" the young lady is in a b
and skirt over a crinoline and wears a hat. Ma
in a bonnet. Papa in a "Tweedside" coat, d
breasted waistcoat and straw hat. (The dog b
love-letter from the "male" in the background
Papa searches the horizon for the orthodox "n
Henry Garland, City of York Art Gallery.

above. 1868. "The Grecian Bend." This
[dro]oping stance, a revival of the post-war mode
[whi]ch had flourished fifty years earlier, was
[mu]ch ridiculed. She wears a short polonaise
bustled behind. *Song Cover.*

330 *above.* 1861. "The Crinoline Dress."
"I've known young ladies dress themselves in waistcoats, coats and hats,
In 'Piccadillies', wide-awakes, and Albert tie cravats.
I never said a single word whichever way they dressed,
But against the use of crinoline I solemnly protest. . . ."
Song Cover.

331 *below left.* 1860. "The Red Petticoat." A looped-up overskirt revealing
the fashionable red petticoat (commonly of flannel) worn over a large cage-
crinoline. Jacket bodice, pork-pie hat and chignon in a hair net. She wears
"Balmoral boots" laced up with red.

"But when with steel hoop the fair owners expand,
Their dresses loop'd up in festoons, oh! 'tis grand!
They seem not to walk—they magestic'ly float
Like swans, on an ocean of red petticoat."
Song Cover.

And presently an observer in 1867 remarked: "We never remember seeing
so many red flannel petticoats in the streets as this winter."

332 *below.* 1861. Fashion Plate. A group of ladies in outdoor garments.
The "Englishwoman's Domestic Magazine".

333. 1862. Youth of fifteen wearing a Tweed-side jacket, buttoned one, and loose trousers. Note watch-chain guard. *Photograph of William T. Webb. See No. 364.*

334. *c.* 1868. A young lady in a Tyrolese hat and figure-fitting paletot (outdoor jacket) over a dress with a pannier skirt. She carries a stick. "There is no dignity or real elegance in the short costume and jacket now worn by fast young ladies who seem to abjure the sweet dignity of woman-hood in a shooting-jacket and a Tyrolese hat." *Original photograph*

335. 1869. Henry Alfred Cunningt wears a very short double-breasted fro coat with broad lapels, and tight trouse the boots have square toes. The "bowle hat with broad brim was becoming serious rival to the tall top hat. *Origi photograph.*

336. 1862. Gentleman in a double-breasted "Chesterfield" overcoat with astrakhan cuffs. This type of overcoat, named after the sixth Earl and distinguished by being slightly waisted and without a seam at the waist, flourished from *c.* 1840 for nearly a hundred years. *Original photograph.*

337. *c.* 1862. An elderly lady in a crinoline skirt somewhat short for walking. Observe the delicacy with which the photographer has arranged that a shadow shall obscure the feet and ankles. *Original photograph.*

338. 1865–8. Gentleman in a sir breasted morning coat, single-brea waistcoat and light check trousers. fashionable "Dundreary" whiskers conspicuous. *Original photograph.*

339. 1862–4. "Seaside Attractions". The young lady in a hat with streamers (known as "follow-me-lads") a blouse with a Swiss belt, appears to be reading *Lady Audley's Secret* (publ. 1862). The young man wears a bowler hat, frock coat, double-breasted waistcoat, light trousers and striped socks. Mama is in a spoon bonnet. *E. Nichols.*

340. *c.* 1862–4. "A Charming Incident". The young women are in hats instead of bonnets, and crinoline dresses; one with a lace shawl, another with a summer jacket. *E. Nichols.*

341 *above left*. 1872. Men's sporting and shooting costu[me?]. The first man is in a Norfolk shirt (becoming known from the 18[…] on as a Norfolk jacket), belted, with matching knickerbockers; [with] this he wears a bowler hat and laced boots. The second man [is in] a lounge coat with flapped pockets, knickerbockers and gai[ters,] straw hat. "*The West End Gazette*".

342 *above right*. 1870. Fashion plate composed of "living per[son]alities"; to wit, Mr. Dickens in a short double-breasted frock [coat,] single-breasted waistcoat, light trousers and top hat; with [Mr.] Disraeli in a suit of "dittos", a single-breasted lounge jacket, o[f the] type known as an Oxonian, buttoned one, and a soft hat. Both [wear] boots with square toes. "*The Tailor & Cutter*", *July* 1870.

343 *left*. 1871. The Dolly Varden costume. After the deat[h of] Dickens the sale of the picture of the heroine in *Barnaby R[udge]* produced a fashion, limited however to the Middle Classes and be[low]. The fashion was a dress made of chintz or the like vaguely i[n] eighteenth-century style. Hence the song:

> "Oh! Have you seen my little girl,
> She doesn't wear a bonnet.
> She's got a monstrous flip-flop hat
> With cherry ribbons on it;
> She dresses in bed furniture
> Just like a flower garden
> A blowin' and a growin'
> And they call it Dolly Varden."

Song Cover.

344 *left*. 1879. Fashion plate. A ball dress with "cuirasse bodice" (i.e. made like a corset), and trained overskirt over a flounced skirt tied back by tapes within. The excessive "tie-back" produced a form of "hobble", the sheath-like dress compelling the scrapping of superfluous underclothing and the introduction of "combinations" which enthusiasts had made of chamois leather. "The modern gown shows the figure in a way perhaps suitable for young and slender people but it is certainly most unsuitable for the ordinary British matron." *"La Mode Parisienne"*.

345 *right*. 1871. Chichester, Lord Carlingford, in a double-breasted morning coat, double-breasted waistcoat and trousers with a narrow stripe, each of different materials. He wears an octagon tie. *J. J. Tissot, Examination Schools, Oxford.*

1871. The University Boat Race. Among the spectators are women in dresses with flounced skirts and draped overskirts; small hats d forward over large chignons of hair at the back of the head. Men are seen in lounge suits with top hats and bowlers or soft felts. Boys are wearing glengarries. *The Parker Gallery.*

348. 1872. Henry Alfred Cunnington. We[ars]
a double-breasted "dress frock coat", [dis]-
tinguished from the ordinary frock coat b[y its]
deeper opening; suitable for more "dre[ss]"
occasions and worn with light trousers. *Ori[ginal]
photograph. See No. 335.*

347 *left. c.* 1877. Group of three children. [The]
boy in a double-breasted jacket and s[hort]
knickerbockers; the girls in Princess polona[ise.]
All three wear elastic-sided boots. *Ori[ginal]
photograph.*

349. 1870. Gentleman in a lounge jacket
("Oxonian"), with knickerbockers and
elastic-sided boots, a costume suitable for
the country. *Original photograph.*

350. 1876. Lady in a Princess polonaise;
the overskirt and bodice were made in
one without a join at the waist. A feature
fashionable that year was the outside
pocket—"now *de rigeur* . . . there could
not be a more convenient arrangement
for a pick-pocket". *Original photograph.*

351. 1872-6. Gentleman in a lo[unge]
morning coat and bowler hat. The [so-]
called "Morning coat" was "the la[test]
adaptation of the old Newmarket riding [coat]
which was so fashionable many years a[go]
and sometimes in the 1870's cut almost [like]
a lounge jacket. *Original photogra[ph.]*

1878–80. Boy in an Eton suit, the jacket and coat braided; a bowler hat in his hand. *Original photograph.*

353. *c.* 1880. Boy in a sailor-suit with bell-bottom trousers. *Original photograph.*

1884. Group of Cambridge Undergraduates. Various styles of ge suits buttoned high with bowler hats. *Original photograph.*

355. 1884. Group of children in a professional photograph. The boys in sailor-suits and holding sailor hats; the girl in a hat with tall crown which when fashionably high was popularly known as "three-storeys and a basement". *Original photograph.*

356 *above*. 1880. Queen Victoria is in an old lady's indoor cap; Princess B is in a boned bodice and draped overskirt with pleated skirt and long seeves. After 1883 the day-sleeves ended well above the wrist. *O photograph*.

357 *top left*. 1885. The Princesses Victoria and Maud as bridesmaids in with sleeves just covering the elbow; hair with high fringed toupee. In fashionable photographs it was customary for the photographer to acce the narrowness of the waist by the deft application of paint on the neg consequently such photographs are not always good evidence of the sm of the waist. *Original photograph*.

358 *left*. 1885. Princess Beatrice in her wedding dress trimmed with abun of "floral attributes". The corset bodice with very short lace sleeves, ma in effect an "evening dress". *Original photograph*.

1884. A family group outside Devizes Castle. The ladies in summer dresses, with tight bodices, high necks, and draped skirts. The married women wear caps. *Original photograph.*

360. 1880. Fashion plate of walking dresses. The trained tie-back has tapes within producing a "hobble" effect. *"Silvia's Home Journal"*.

361. 1886. Fashion Plate of Outdoor Costumes. Th view of Dolman-Pelisses indicate the size of bustl

362. 1888. Fashion Plate of a lady in "Eton jacket". *"The Tailor & Cutter"*, August 2nd, 1888.

363. 1889. Men's Outdoor Costume, showing an I ness with cape, and a double-breasted Cheste overcoat. *"The West End Gazette"*.

886. Mr. and Mrs. William T. Webb. The husband in a
͏e suit of one material; his wife in a dress with tight-fitting
͏e, shortened sleeves then fashionable, and long ribbon
͏ming of two colours. *Original photograph: see No.* 333.

365. *c.* 1884. Husband and wife. He is in a morning coat
buttoned high, low collar and small lapels. His wife wears
a polonaise dress with extensive gauging, then very fashionable. Her hat with tall domed crown. *Original photograph.*

889. Mrs. W. T. Webb and children. Mother in severely
dress. Little boy on her knee "shortened" from long
clothes. *Original photograph.*

367. *c.* 1883. The husband in a morning coat; his wife in a
tight high-necked bodice.

368 *above*. 1885. The lady singing wears an eve[ning] dress with an immense bustle and long train. At [this] state the bustle had reached its maximum size [so] that a large tea-tray could rest upon it. "*Illust[rated] London News*", *July* 27, 1885.

369 *left*. 1889. Mrs. Henschel in a day dress o[f two] materials, with sleeves showing the fashionable "[mount] up" at the shoulder. *Original photograph.*

370 *left*. 1887. Fashion plate of two evening dr[esses] with a day dress in the centre. The bustles an[d the] excess of drapery—and tight lacing—were ch[arac]-teristic of the period when, acording to [an] enthusiastic critic "never was the art of wor[nen's] dress so brilliantly carried out as in the present [day]." "*Weldon's Fashions*".

An American comment in 1883: "Englishwome[n are] the worst dressed, except perhaps the Ger[mans.] Good taste is conspicuous by its absence; in for[m the] English dress is dowdy, and in colour frigh[tful...]

371 *above*. 1890. The Duchess of Connaught. Family group. The mother in a tailor-made coat and skirt with a waistcoat bodice. The children in kilts and Scotch caps. *Original photograph.*

372 *top left*. 1889–90. The earliest form of a gentleman's "dinner jacket", at first called a "dress jacket", worn open with a silk-faced rolled collar. Known in U.S.A. as a "tuxedo".

373 *left*. 1891. Lady Colin Campbell in an afternoon dress of the "blouse and skirt" style. The blouse is accordion-pleated and overhangs the plain skirt. The sleeves of the style then becoming fashionable. *Original photograph.*

374 *top left*. 1891–2. Outdoor costumes. The gentleman i
new style of overcoat, shaped like a "top frock" and
fronted; like a Chesterfield but three inches longer. The
is in a double-breasted Chesterfield, and carries a small
of the fashionable size. "*The Tailor & Cutter*".

375 *above*. 1891. Sporting costumes. "The Norfolk dres
both ladies and gents." ("*Tailor & Cutter*", *June* 1891.)
skirt is now plain and has lost the drapery of the prec
decade. "The enthusiasm with which the perfectly plain
was welcomed shows clearly which way English taste lies"
cit.). "Walking skirts are now of a sensible length and width,
three and a half yards wide and only reaching to the a
or even a little above." "*The Tailor & Cutter*".

376 *left*. 1891. Summer costume. The lady in a jacket and w
coat and plain skirt, tailor-made; "the gent's collar and t
to make a dress perfect and complete." The gentleman i
covert coat which can be worn alone or as an overcoat cov
a short lounge jacket. "*The Tailor & Cutter*".

right. 1890. Miss Agnes Huntington in a day dress of two materials, "corselet" body, tight sleeves, and skirt still slightly draped. She wears a small toque with upright trimming. *Original photograph.*

bottom right. 1892. Miss Marion Lea in a coat and waistcoat over a blouse with a masculine collar and tie. She wears a small hat tied under the chin. *Original photograph.*

below. c. 1892. Lady Randolph Churchill in evening dress with square *étage*, round waist, puffed elbow sleeves and the fashionable broad lace revers. *Original photograph.*

380. 1895. "Four Generations", middle class. The great-grandfather, seated, wears an old-fashioned double-breasted frock-coat. The grandfather, standing, has a three-button lounge-morning coat with lapelled waistcoat. The young mother has the fashionable gigot sleeve with revers over the shoulder. The baby is in a shortened frock. *Original photograph.*

1894. A Royal Group of four generations. Queen Victoria in a widow's cap; the baby in long clothes was the future Duke of Windsor.
...ding, in frock coat with octagon ties, the Prince of Wales (later Edward VII) and the Duke of York (later George V). *Original photograph.*

382. 1894. Fashion plate of four ladies. (1) Coat and skirt; the former with wide revers and leg-of-mutton sleeves worn over a shirt with masculine collar and tie. (2) A shoulder wrap of net trimmed with jet and steel beads. (3) A navy-blue serge dress trimmed with black braid edged with scarlet; leg-of-mutton sleeves; gored skirt. (4) A golf-cape with straps and lined with plaid. All the hats are trimmed with feathers or flowers. The golf costume might have the skirt as much as six inches off the ground, worn with cloth knickerbockers and gaiters. *"The Lady"*.

383. 1896. An evening dress of black accordion-pleated tulle over a pink foundation; large ballooned sleeves long gloves reaching above the elbows. The bow on the shoulder and the waistband with a bow were the height fashion. *"The Gentlewoman"*.

384 *left*. 1894. Ladies' Riding Habits. The single- and the double-breasted were equally fashionable. Trained skirts persisted in spite of attempts to introduce the un-trained. Under the skirt trousers had replaced the white petticoat since the 1870s. A top hat was generally worn in town; a jockey cap sometimes in the country, for hunting. *"The West End Gazette"*.

385 *right*. 1895–1900. The "New Woman" in bicycling costume. The feature was the knickerbockers, sometimes called "rationals". The coat "gracefully defines the figure while the full skirt, dropping just below the seat behind and falling on the knickers in front is the best substitute that could be had for the full length skirt. There does not seem anything unladylike in it. . . . The knickers and leggings complete the dress." *The Tailor & Cutter*," March, 1895.

386. 1924. Motoring and sports coats. The coats long, ample and shapeless with straight lines, roll collars or wide turn-overs. Walking shoes often having two straps. *Radio Times Hulton Picture Library.*

PART SIX

The Twentieth Century

The Edwardian man-about-town carried on the traditions of the dandy, the beau, and the buck under increasing difficulties, economic and social. The frightful burden of shilling income tax and the democratic intrusion of all classes into outdoor sports combined to obliterate those niceties of dress which had distinguished the Gentleman from the Not-quite.

The Gentleman's exclusive day was drawing to an end in a glowing sunset, and until the fateful August 1914 his fashions remained essentially unchanged, though the frock coat was giving way to the morning coat, while the lounge suit, especially in striped flannel, was encroaching on the domains of both. The waist was somewhat short and trousers on the narrow side (18-inch knee, 17-inch bottoms).

The white slip within the waistcoat of the morning coat or frock coat remained fashionable, and with these button boots with suede tops were preferred to laced boots. The increasing taste for motoring, however, was replacing the silk hat by the Homburg and encouraging the sack overcoat in place of the fitting Chesterfield. By 1912 the bottoms of the trouser legs in lounge suits were permanently turned up, a habit borrowed from the Lower Orders and now a sign of the times.

The war of 1914 to 1918 paralysed male fashions, and at its conclusion all that survived was "a costume of dull drab monotony and severe cut and outline that offends the aesthetic faculty and repels and depresses" (*The Tailor & Cutter*). Two important casualties of the war were the frock coat, described in 1921 as "dead as the Dodo", and the silk hat, both becoming curios hired for special functions.

On the other hand, novelties such as the Fair Isle pullover sought to add colour, and in that year the golfer's knickerbockers began to pouch and sag, becoming by 1925 the voluminous "plus-fours", the material pleated into a waistband as in the trousers of lounge suits. As women's legs became more exposed, men's became more and more muffled in trousers, 22 inches at the knee and 19-inch bottoms, the extreme form known as "Oxford Bags" in 1927 being even 24 inches round the bottoms.

All through this decade spats were worn in Town with Morning coats, but in spite of attempts to persuade a livelier iris to blossom on the burnish'd dove "there is a wave of shabbiness sweeping over the country . . . due to a revolution in social conditions" (*The Tailor & Cutter*, November 1925). The cost of good clothing had risen beyond the means of many; yet an attempt in 1921 to introduce "Standard Suits" at £4 10s. failed. Apparently even the Common Man did not want to look exactly like everyone else.

Between the two wars the principal change was in the direction of discarding superfluous garments; hats, waistcoats and gloves were often omitted, and formal costume for special occasions was hired. As such it ceased to express the wearer's personal taste.

We are too close to the Second World War of 1939-45 to be able to estimate its full effect on male costume beyond the obvious decline in sartorial importance of the Man-about-Town. We have to look, instead, at the modes favoured by a much wider social group uncertain at present whether to go forward or backward.

Feminine fashions of the Edwardian period reached a high degree of technical skill in elaborate designs exploiting curves both natural and artificial. The spirit was decorously sensual, aided by erotic lingerie foaming about the feet. It was a style which favoured the mature woman, an impressive resistance against the audacities of the New Woman.

From 1909, however, the ideal "fashion age" began to recede and the close-fitting tubular dress and hobble skirt implied that youth was in the ascendant. During the 1914-18 war, with many young women in the Services or engaged in war-work, the Hobble gave place to a more practical skirt, and with it appeared the coat-frock and the jumper.

Post-war fashions announced that women had become still more juvenile and aimed at resembling schoolboys— "such enchanting, sexless, bosomless, hipless, thighless creatures"—with short hair and no waists, in frock barely reaching the knees.

A return to femininity, beginning in 1925, introduced a schoolgirl shape with even a hint of a return to the "figure", culminating in 1929 with "Fashion's new discovery that the feminine form is lovely". Body-worship became the mode, expressed by slimming, nudity, skin-tanning, face-painting and the technique of the films.

The spirit of class-distinction had been effectively exorcised; sex appeal resorted to its most democratic form, nudity, lavishly displayed in the backless evening dress. You were told in 1938 that "you can be unbelievably alluring in the sheathlike evening frock", but the very next year there were other things to think about; a magazine of 1892 had foretold that "in fifty years women will be wearing trousers", and in 1942 the prophecy came true with a vengeance.

In the main wartime fashions were summed up in the words: "We make do with what we have". Not until 1949, when controls were finally removed, did all garments become "coupon-free". All those years women had waited with impatient expectancy for some original fashion to express the new era and its ideas. Alas! The "New Look" proved to be merely another revival, this time of a dull mode of the 1880's. If the art of costume is to survive as an art expressing the ideas of the day, and not become merely an industry, the modern woman is surely not to be fobbed off with revivals!

Down the centuries costume fashions have reflected the tastes of whatever social group dominated the community; at first an exclusive group, but gradually expanding until it included the middle class. Now, after the war, it has spread farther still, and fashions must reflect the ideas of that nebulous entity known as the Common Man. It is he who will determine the future of the art of costume.

387. 1905-6. Radlett Tennis Club, showing tennis costumes. *From a photograph.*

388. 1900. Fashion plate of two ladies in outdoor costumes. One is in a loose reefer-style coat, fly-fronted, with flapped ticket pocket. The other in a figure-fitting double-breasted jacket. The skirts have a slight flare. "*The West End Gazette*".

389. 1901. Fashion plate of ladies' coats. 1. A three-quarter outdoor coat, figure-fitting. 2. A short jacket which with the skirt forms a "coat and skirt" suit. The skirts are flared. "*The West End Gazette*".

390. 1901. Fashion plate showing men's overcoats. A frock coat (which could be worn without an under-coat). A loose double-breasted Chesterfield. "*The West End Gazette*".

391. 1901. Group of children. 1. Boy in a lounge suit. "At this age they have almost forgotten the existence of sailor suits . . . their ambition is to be men." 2. A girl in a loose-fitting double-breasted coat. 3. An Eton suit. "The Eton jacket is to the boy what the frock coat is to the swell" (*loc. cit.*). "*The West End Gazette*".

392. 1901. Five young men. Note the
high stand collars, worn with a varie
of neckties; the new style of doubl
breasted waistcoat with the butto
forming a V. Two are wearing cumme
bunds in place of waistcoats, a fashi
first introduced in 1893 from Ind
Original photograph.

393. 1907. Lady's motoring costume. An
ample motor coat, worn with a fur toque
with flaps. "*The Ladies' Tailor*".

394. 1907. Fashion plate of Gentleman's
Tennis Costume. "*The Tailor & Cutter*".

395. 1907. Fashion plate of lady's
ing costume. A jacket with short sle
tight waist, and very flared trained
small toque. The front hair is raised a
the forehead with pads and back brus
"*The Ladies' Tailor*".

1907–8. Miss Margaret Leslie.
...oon gown. "The lingerie
... almost beggar description, so
...site are they in their filmy
...ess." *Radio Times Hulton
Picture Library*.

397 *left. c.* 1903. Lady with parasol. Wearing a visiting dress trimmed with velvet bows; fashionable flat-crowned hat worn tilted forwards. *Radio Times Hulton Picture Library.*

398 *below.* 1910. Three ladies at Cowes. Wearing coat and skirt costumes and large hats. "Mammoth shapes, the crowns the size of dinner plates and rather low, and brims either extinguishing or turning up a trifle at the back . . . craze for extravagant veils." *Radio Times Hulton Picture Library.*

1908. A fashionable teagown. "I do not think that any of us can exist at any time of the year without a teagown." *Radio Times Hulton Picture Library*.

400 *left.* 1911. Fashion plate of gentleman's seaside fashions. A suit of "flannels", a double-breasted coat and trousers in striped flannel. Note the trouser legs turned up at the bottom, the correct mode except with frock coat or morning coat. Note the straw "boater" hat. *"The Tailor & Cutter"*.

401 *right.* 1914. Gentleman's smart lounge suit; single-breasted coat, the trousers with front crease well-marked; the bottoms turned up. *"The Tailor & Cutter"*.

402 and 403 *below left.* 1914. The pre-war Hobble skirt. Long skirts extremely narrow round the hem, worn with cutaway coats. *"The Ladies' Tailor"*.

404 *below right.* 1916. Male evening dress. The Gentleman and the Waiter. The chief distinction appears to have been the metal buttons on the latter's coat. *"The Tailor & Cutter"*.

405 *top left*. 1916. Ladies' tailor-made coats and short full skirts. Worn with high buttoned boots with suede or cloth tops. "*The Ladies' Tailor*".

406 *top right*. 1918. Two coats and skirts made in the "barrel line", an attempt to give the outline of a barrel from neck to hem; a style introduced in 1916, but becoming a marked fashion in 1918. "*The Royal Catalogue of Ladies' Fashions*".

407 *left*. 1917. Coat-Frocks. The "all-in-one" frock, or the "coat-gown" as the tailors prefer to call it, came into fashion in 1916 but it was soon better known as a "coat-frock", a term continuing into 1921. The long pleats and outside pockets were features. "*The Ladies' Tailor*".

408 *above*. 1924. Fashions shown at British Empire Exhibition by the Bradford Chamber of Commerce. Five Models. Afternoon frocks, very plain and flat front and back. "The accredited thing is to have no waist." Short hair. "To shingle or not to shingle is much discussed." Afternoon shoes with one strap. *Radio Times Hulton Library*.

409 *left*. 1920. Women's Coats and Skirts.
"If the modern woman powders her nose in season and out of season, she at least does not tight lace". "*The Ladies' Tailor*".

410 *right*. 1921–2. Lounge suits. "*Grafton Fashions*".

411. 1920. A dance frock. With pannier drapery and a wide sash reaching across the hips. *Radio Times Hulton Picture Library*.

412 *above left*. 1926. Seaside costume. "The two-pice costume again dominates the mo
The summer mode "is to be simple and youthful". The costume is embroidered and v
with a cloche hat. *Radio Times Hulton Picture Library.*

413 *above right*. 1926. Evening dress. Sleeveless and hanging in straight lines. Of c
d'or, gold embroidered. *Radio Times Hulton Picture Library.*

414 *left*. 1928. Female bathing costume of the period consisting of a substantial tunic
knickers. *Original photograph.*

415. 1924. Afternoon dresses. Short with a waistline round the hips; cloche hats. A large bunch of artificial flowers on the shoulder very fashionable. *Radio Times Hulton Picture Library*.

416. 1924. Gentleman's double-breasted reefer-lounge suit. The coat is short-waisted and the turned-up trousers are narrow. Worn with spats. *"The Tailor & Cutter"*.

417. 1927. Ladies' outdoor costumes. Coat with low waist and short pleated skirt. The second figure shows a long coat ending just above the skirt hem. Both wear cloche hats. *"The Tailor and Cutter"*.

418. 1927. Gentleman's Lounge Suit double-breasted reefer coat, short-waist with striped trousers and spats. It is n worthy that at this period while the m waist-level was short the female was tremely low. *"The Tailor & Cutter"*

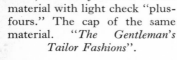

419. 1928. Man's Golfing costume, a short jacket in a dark material with light check "plus-fours." The cap of the same material. *"The Gentleman's Tailor Fashions"*.

420. 1928. Man's Riding Costume, worn with jodpurs. *"The Tailor & Cutter"*.

421. 1928. Lounge suit. *" Gentleman's Tailor Fashions*

422 *above*. 1930. Evening gown. Longer skirts had become fashionable; the bodice with shoulder-straps cut in with it; the waist is marked by a belt. Material is fancy tinsel chiffon. *Radio Times Hulton Picture Library.*

423 *above left*. 1930. Evening gown. In gold lamé without a belt. *Radio Times Hulton Picture Library.*

424 *left*. 1930. Backless evening dress with shoulder straps, the skirt close-fitting. Short hair. *Original photograph.*

425. 1932–3. Outdoor costume. A winter overcoat in dark blue wool with a grey fur collar; the coat slightly waisted. The hat typical of the period. *Radio Times Hulton Picture Library.*

426. 1930. Mr. and Mrs. Ray. "Going-away" costume; a bride and bridegroom of 1930. *Original photograph.*

428 *bottom right.* 1930. Sports wear. A blue silk suit with a fancy check jumper; the hat is a modification of the cloche with the narrow brim turned up away from the face but descending deeply behind. *Radio Times Hulton Picture Library.*

427. 1931–2. Sea-faring suit. She w a blue coat and beige slacks of the s worn earlier by men and known "Oxford bags". *Radio Times Hr Picture Library.*

429. 1936–8. Golfer in long "plus-fours" and sleeveless pullover. *Original photograph.*

430. 1934. Two young girls in seaside "play-suits". *Original photograph.*

31. 1935. Summer dresses at the Eton and Harrow Cricket Match. A long lace coat with barrel sleeves and a deep flat collar. The summer hat has a shallow crown and wide brim which is made to dip over one eye, a fashion of this year. *Radio Times Hulton Picture Library.*

432 *above*. 1938. Evening gown. A "pillar-s
satin evening gown which "clings to the
like a wet cloth". Sleeveless and with a s
train. *Radio Times Hulton Picture Lib*

433 *left*. 1934. Evening dress. "Back intere
ubiquitous". A deep V-shaped back ope
edged with "drapery frills". The skirt cut o
bias. *Radio Times Hulton Picture Library*

434 *below*. 1947. Sport and seaside costume,
shorts in Bedford cord. Note the hair style.
Gallery of English Costume, Platt Hall, Manche

435 *left.* 1948. Beach dress and play suit in zig-zag pattern known as "tidal wave". *The Gallery of English Costume, Platt Hall, Manchester.*

436 *right.* 1949. Day dress showing a return to the constricted waist. *The Gallery of English Costume, Platt Hall, Manchester.*

437 *bottom left.* 1947. "The New Look" with the "washerwoman skirt". *The Gallery of English Costume, Platt Hall, Manchester.*

438 *bottom centre.* 1940–1. Gentleman's smart lounge suit for winter wear. *"The Tailor & Cutter" Supplement.*

439 *bottom right.* 1949. Evening dress moulding the figure with a trained back-panel to suggest some fullness. The width at the top helps to accentuate the narrowness of the waist. *The Gallery of English Costume, Platt Hall, Manchester.*

440. 1948. Mr. and Mrs. Luckham showing lounge suit and tailor-made costume of the period.

441. 1948. H.R.H. the Duke of Edinburgh and Princess Elizabeth, showing lounge suit and tailor-made costume.

Acknowledgements

The authors and publishers would like to acknowledge gratefully the following sources from which reproductions have been taken. References throughout this list are to numbers of plates.

Allbrook, A. F., 2
Agnew, Thomas, & Sons, 212, 249

Bacon, Sir Edmund, 88
Bearsted, Viscount, 194
Bedford, Duke of, 96
Birmingham City Art Gallery, 191, 200, 201, 217, 317, 327
Bodleian Library, Oxford, 8, 11, 15, 168
Bolton, Lord, 81
Bradford City Art Gallery, 227
British Museum, 4–7, 9, 10, 12, 13, 17, 20, 35, 38, 42, 43, 49, 52, 80, 113, 162, 174.

Chaworth-Masters, Col. J. N., 232
Cheltenham Museum, 301
Christchurch Mansion, Ipswich, 123, 133, 164, 177, 185
Colchester Corporation, 183
Compton, Major Edward, 260
Corpus Christi College, Cambridge, 18, 19
Courtauld Institute of Art, 59, 107, 155, 187

Eton College, 43
Exeter Cathedral, Dean and Chapter of, 47

Fitzwilliam, the Earl, 83, 123

Gallery of English Costume, Platt Hall, Manchester, 437–4, 439

Heaton, Wallace, Ltd., (Photographers), 203
Hereford Cathedral, Dean and Chapter of, 14
Hind, Arthur M., 71, 109, 110
Hughes, Dr. John B., 246

Kenyon, Lord, 73
Knoedler & Co., 220

Leeds City Art Gallery and Temple Newsam House, 1, 186, 195, 196, 202

Leger J., and Sons, 251
Leggatt Bros., 205, 223
Leicester City Art Gallery, 216, 262
Leathes, Lieutenant-Commander Robert, R.N., 180

Macdonald-Buchanan, Major and the Hon., 175
Magdalene College, Cambridge, 36, 37
Manchester City Art Gallery, 138, 313, 317
Mountain, Sir Brian, 193
Mountbatten of Burma, the late Countess, 129

National Buildings Record, 78, 118
National Gallery of Ireland, 198

National Galleries of Scotland, 69, 190, 245, 263
National Portrait Gallery, 62, 67, 68, 79, 86, 103, 120, 128, 172, 188, 255
Neville, Hon. R. C., 64, 70, 75, 76, 77, 84, 104
Normanton, the Earl of, 261
Norwich Castle Museum, 136, 159, 173, 208
Nottingham City Art Gallery, 211, 236

Oxford, Faculty of Music, 90

Parker Gallery, 346
Peterborough Museum, 114, 117
Petre, Lord, Ingatestone Hall, 74, 102, 108, 134
Pitcher, Sidney (Photographer), 55, 105
Preston, Harris Art Gallery, 204

H.M. the Queen, 63, 66, 106

Radio Times Hulton Picture Library, 386, 396–9, 411–13, 415, 422, 423, 425, 427, 428, 431–3

Rothermere, Lord, 122
Royal Academy of Arts, 72, 222, 345
Royal Albert Memorial Museum, Exeter, 156, 199, 215, 270
Rylands Library, Manchester, 54

Salisbury, Marquess of, 87
Scotsman Publications Ltd., 56
Shirley, Hon. Andrew, 121
Spink, C. Marshall, 203
Sykes, Sir Richard, 242

Tailor & Cutter, The, seventeen plates from 1870–1940/1
Tate Gallery, 207, 221, 226, 229, 230
Tooth Galleries, 209, 210, 213, 225, 228, 235

University College, Oxford, 82

Vansittart-Neale, Miss P., 85
Victoria and Albert Museum, 53, 92, 119, 129, 160, 268, 299

Walker Art Gallery, Liverpool, 189, 218, 224, 241, 312
Washington and Lee University, Virginia, USA, 234
Wickham-Boynton, Marcus, 132
Winchelsea and Nottingham, the Earl of, 91
Windham, Lieutenant-Commander C., 250
Wombwell, Captain V. E. M., 206
Worsley, Sir William, 98

Yarborough, the Earl of, 97
York City Art Gallery, 142, 214